JOSEF GOLDBRUNNER

TEACHING
THE SACRAMENTS

PENANCE

EUCHARIST

CONFIRMATION

HERDER AND HERDER

HERDER AND HERDER, NEW YORK
232 Madison Avenue, New York 16, N.Y.

Original edition "Sakramentenunterricht mit dem Werkheft", Kösel, Munich
Translation and American edition by Eva Fleischner

5th impression: 1964

CONTENTS

Confirmation

PREFACE TO THE AMERICAN EDITION

This translation has been prepared from the fifth, and completely revised German edition of *Sakramentenunterricht,* for use in the third or fourth grades. In collaboration with the author, who has repeatedly lectured and taught in the United States, a number of changes and adaptations have been made in the text in order to render it more usable in American schools. It is hoped that this American edition will meet with the same wide success as the original edition has done.

Grailville   *Eva Fleischner*

TEACHING RELIGION WITH THE WORKBOOK

There are several advantages, both in the classroom and at home, that result when children keep a workbook. In the *classroom,* the catechist is obliged not only to speak during the lesson, but also to write and draw on the board. Thus he addresses himself to the children's eyes as well as to their ears. The diagram which takes shape gradually on the board helps the children to concentrate, reinforces the lesson by making clear its structure, high-lights key phrases, and, through the drawing, gives direction to the imagination.

It has also been found from experience that children like to work at their workbooks *at home.* As a rule, they are already familiar with keeping a workbook from other subjects. But in religious instruction more scope can be given them as regards lay-out and color. The interest, diligence and enthusiasm which often result from this prove how good it is to be able to give pictorial expression to one's spiritual life. Moreover, many a catechist has come to appreciate the influence of the workbook on the child's family. The novelty of this kind of religious instruction often appeals strongly to parents of an older generation, who begin to follow the work with interest. This can act as a sort of review for them, especially if the child explains drawings and text to them. We should not underestimate this missionary effect of the workbook.

The drawings themselves should conform to specific requirements. They should be drawn quickly, with simple strokes of the chalk. For this reason no use is made of perspective and human figures, while the ancient Christian symbols again come into their own.

The choice of color is left to the catechist's imagination -- the reaction of the children will guide him. In the case of children who are capable of working independently, the small symbolic drawing on the board will often serve merely as an incentive or point of contact for drawings which express a genuine experience. The catechist should foster creativity and originality in the children as much as possible.

No fixed rule as to the exact moment when the diagram should be drawn during class can be given. It will differ from one class to the next, and will depend on the catechist's temperament, or on unexpected interruptions, such as questions or objections that may be raised. Sometimes it will be best to teach the entire lesson without interruption, and to draw the diagram only at the end, as summary. A more abstract lesson, on the other hand, may call for the diagram as starting point. In the case of inexperienced teachers, it is in general advisable to put the diagram on the board gradually, as the lesson progresses: title – key word which has been explained – drawing (= D) – key phrase (T = text). The catechist must be thoroughly prepared for his class, and should not deviate from the main points of the lesson. At least five minutes before the end of class he should give the children time to take down the diagram, quickly and in rough form, on a pad or sheet of paper. Only at home are they to copy it into their workbook, carefully and in color. Concentrated teaching on the part of the catechist will more than make up for the five minutes thus "lost".

The workbook in religious instruction makes use of the new – and at the same time old – principle of "learning by doing": whatever is taught and explained should also in some way be "done". For doing demands a transference of what has been heard, so that the material which has been received by the intellect is now brought into contact with the whole man. His imagination, will, decision, diligence, emotions, creativity, etc., are all brought into play. When we *do* something we are required to make the content our own to a greater degree than when we merely memorize it. The percentage of children who follow the lesson purely mechanically is thus reduced, so that the principle of learning by doing, of which the workbook is *one* application, can be said to serve the concrete realization of our spiritual life.

The lessons in this book are based on the following principles:

1. They contain all that is essential for each sacrament, so that as the children grow older, they can continue to build on this foundation.

2. The pastoral-theological starting point throughout is the *form* of the sacrament, which enables us to penetrate into the interior *event* (confession = court-trial; eucharist = communal meal; confirmation = anointing for a task). The definition and completion of this early teaching is the task of religious instruction in the upper grades.

3. The simple and childlike style should at all times do justice to the lofty content. Later development will be possible only if the world which has been constructed in these early years was not a childish world.

The Sacrament of Penance

1. The lessons on the sacrament of penance here given build on what the children have experienced since their first confession, and attempt to deepen their knowledge and to bring it into the proper order. The deepening is aimed at the mystery of the sacrament, but also at moral teaching suitable for children in the third and fourth grades. The examination of conscience in the first two grades should deal with questions that belong to the world of children: at home – at play – in school – in church.

2. The sacrament of penance is presented throughout under the image of a court-trial. Each individual detail is arranged according to what happens at such a trial: confessional – judgment seat; confessor – judge; penitent – accused; confession of sins – accusation; exhortation – talking with the judge; absolution – verdict; penance – reparation.

3. The morality of the grade-school child is a morality of obedience; now is the time to learn, to form habits and customs. This will make itself felt also in the child's spiritual life, especially in his reception of the sacraments. Although confession is an eminently personal act – an encounter with God and a free decision – this personal aspect will not assume the leading role during childhood. Instead, the main emphasis will be given to the correct performance of external actions, which are permeated with obedience-morality and with newly acquired knowledge; they will be more or less personal, depending on the child's degree of maturity. Our main task at this stage, therefore, is to equip him with a solid "scaffolding" to which he will gradually become accustomed, so that the force of habit will help him overcome a possible crisis in later life.

The headings of the examination of conscience and the "five steps" of confession provide the majority of Catholics with all that they need to know about the sacrament. They may be compared to rails, along which even the clumsiest can once again find his way back to the confessional with relative ease, if God gives the grace. On the other hand, the scaffolding must allow room for the individual formulation of the confession of sins – indeed, it should call for it. This is achieved by omitting the questions of the typical examination of conscience, which only pave the way for mechanical confession.

4. The moral maturing of man demands that his instruction on penance be continued. If Christians never outgrow their childhood dress in the reception of this sacrament, confession will degenerate into routine and barter; while this may be excusable in the case of the child, who is not yet capable of fully personal acts, it gives scandal to God and to man. It is the important task confronting adolescence and maturity to make confession into that personal act in which the human being awakens more and more. From the very first, our teaching on penance must contain in germ the full potential for further growth.

MERCIFUL JUDGMENT

AIM. To make clear what takes place in confession by comparing it with the procedure at a court-trial, and to work out the structure of confession in five steps.

PREPARATION. Today we are going to talk about a very special chair. A chair is made to be sat in – when we eat, when we talk or read. Now there are certain kinds of chairs in which only very special people sit, and whenever they do so it has a special meaning: e.g., the king seats himself on a chair called "throne", while his subjects stand before him; he is the one who has power and rules. The bishop and the pope also sit on a throne. (What would it be like if Jesus had his throne here among us?) In our churches there is still another kind of special chair, and it can become very important in the life of each of us: the judgment seat (T).

PRESENTATION. The judge is seated – before him stand the accuser and the accused. The judge listens to the one, cross-examines the other, and tests their evidence. Then he weighs the words of each. As with a pair of scales, he places the offense on one side of the scales and the punishment on the other, until the scales are balanced and the punishment is just. Then he pronounces the verdict. He must judge justly, even when it is hard to do so. Even if the accused pleads for mercy, justice must be done.

EXPLANATION. 1. In our church too there stands a judgment seat! It is a real judgment seat, but it has another name: "confessional" (T and diagram).

2. Who is the judge? The priest. He listens, cross-examines, tests the truth of what is said, and pronounces the verdict. This judge has a special name, "confessor" (T). We call him "Father", as

though he were not only severe like a judge, but kind and helpful like a father! The accused is called "penitent" (T).

3. Who is the accuser in the confessional? We ourselves. And the accused? Also we ourselves. Is it not strange that someone should accuse himself? Ordinarily people don't like to do this, but in the confessional they do it freely, of their own accord. There must be some special reason for this.

4. They admit their guilt and place it on one side of the scales; but before doing so they ask God to forgive them and promise to be better in the future. And what happens now? What is placed on the other side of the scales? Punishment? No – something else, something mysterious, good and wonderful, a gift: it is called "mercy". (We shall hear later who it is that gives us this gift.) That is why the judgment in the confessional is called "merciful judgment" (title).

5. And now the priest pronounces the verdict, it is called "absolution" (T). Do you think that the penitent leaves the confessional in a happy frame of mind? Yes, happy and free – and grateful? Grateful to whom? To the one who gave him this gift of mercy, to God in heaven.

6. Going to confession is both difficult and easy. You have been doing it for some time already, but now you must learn to understand it better. You must become familiar with five steps (the Roman numerals are added to the diagram), and must understand their meaning: three beforehand, one in the confessional, and one afterwards. (While saying this the catechist points to the diagram, to help the children to identify each step.)

I. I, the accuser, consider what my sins are. I look into my soul to see where there is sin in it. This is called "examination of conscience" (T).

14

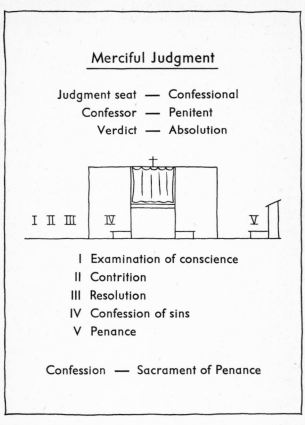

Merciful Judgment

Judgment seat — Confessional
Confessor — Penitent
Verdict — Absolution

I Examination of conscience
II Contrition
III Resolution
IV Confession of sins
V Penance

Confession — Sacrament of Penance

II. I, the accused, ask for forgiveness. This is the most difficult of the five steps, but it is also the most important one. It is called "contrition" (T).

III. I, the accused, promise and make up my mind to be better from now on. This is called "resolution" (T).

IV. Now I enter the confessional and accuse myself. I confess my sins. This is called "confession of sins" (T).

V. After the wonderful verdict of the "absolution" I kneel down in a pew in church, to thank God and to perform a task which the priest has given me. This fifth step is called "penance" (T).

You must learn these five steps very thoroughly. They are like a railing to which we can hold on in the dark so as to find our way, so that we know what to do. We say of someone who performs all the steps in the right order that he "goes to confession" (T), or, he receives the "sacrament of penance" (T). We shall be studying each of the five steps in turn, so that you will understand the meaning of each.

APPLICATION. What would it be like if this judgment seat – this merciful judgment of confession – did not exist? Nevermore mercy – only just punishment! Now you can understand what a great gift Jesus gave us on Easter Sunday, when he instituted the sacrament of penance. When you see the confessional in church next Sunday, look at it with gratitude in your heart.

AIM. Moral teaching for children is shown to be a means of finding the road to God.

PREPARATION. Each of you often takes the same road, e.g., the road to school, or to church. This road has a beginning (home), and a goal (school or church). Maybe you walk or ride along it a quarter of an hour, or half an hour at the most.

Today we shall draw a road which is different for each person. It lasts our whole life, it is the "road" of our life. Where do we want to get to? The goal must be beautiful, good and great, bright and shining, so that we shall set out full of joy. The road of our life is something like the road up a mountain (diagram). When the sun sets behind it (diagram) it looks as though, once we are at the top, we could leap right into the light.

We know that this is not possible, but it is something like this with the road of our life.

EXPLANATION. 1. What shall we call the goal? Heaven – gate of heaven – "God." So the title will be: "My road to God" (T).

2. All sorts of things can happen on such a road. Sometimes we march along rapidly, because we enjoy walking; sometimes we are tired; or there is suddenly a thick fog, so that we no longer see where the road is going. What can help us then? A compass? Yes, each of us carries one in his heart. It is called "conscience", you will learn more about it when you are older. And a map? Yes, that is the holy Bible. As you grow up you will learn to read it yourselves. But there is something else as well which helps us to find the right road. Along this road there are ten signposts. On the front of each are written ten headings or points, and on the back of each there is a sentence which begins with the words: "God wants us to. . .".

17

3. These signposts tell us exactly what God wants of us and how we are to live. If we pay attention to each and follow the direction in which it points, we shall find the road to God and shall reach our goal.

4. But suppose we go in the other direction, even though the words "God wants us to . . ." are written on the signpost? If we don't do what God wants, then the road of our life runs in the wrong direction. And if we keep going in the wrong direction we shall arrive one day – not at the gate of heaven, but at the gate of hell. So you see that if we do not follow one of the signposts, we commit a sin. To sin is to go astray, to take the wrong road, a road which leads to unhappiness.

APPLICATION. How long will the road of our life last? 70 years perhaps, or 80, or 90 years – we don't know how long. The road of life of some people is short, they reach the goal already when they are 50 or 40 years old; others have less time still. None of us knows whether he is still at the beginning of the road (point to the diagram), or close to its end.

But one thing we all should know: does the road of our life go in the direction of the light? Jesus has told us that he is the "light of the world", and that anyone who follows him will not go astray. Listen to his words, later you can write them into your workbook (this can be the closing prayer):

> "I am the light of the world.
> He who follows me does not walk in darkness."
>
> (John 8:12)

My Road to God

He who follows me
does not walk in darkness.

1. LIVING WITH GOD

AIM. The vast realm of man's interior relationship with God (= living with God) is experienced by children in their prayer life. The first signpost, therefore, forms part of the teaching on prayer.
PREPARATION. With whom do you talk most often? Let us suppose – with your mother. It is different all the time: sometimes there are questions – sometimes you ask her for something – sometimes you tell her about all sorts of things. (The catechist should give typical examples of one sentence each, without getting lost in them!) And mother: she answers your questions – gives you what you ask for – refuses it – tells you things in her turn; or, she scolds you – is angry – praises you. It is different from day to day. But there are some days when she does not talk to you at all. Maybe she is angry, or sad. When that happens you are very worried. Then *you* begin to talk to her. And so there is a constant back-and-forth. This is what living with mother is like. Is it possible to live like this with someone we don't see? We don't see God, and yet we are meant to talk with him always, i.e., to pray. Not only do we not see him, but we cannot even hear his voice; and yet, we are meant to live in this way with God (T: Living with God). This is written on the front of signpost No. 1. On the back is written: "God wants us to listen to him, to think of him gladly, and to pray fervently" (T). To pray to him, every day, this is not easy. There is a wrong way of doing it, and a right way.
PRESENTATION AND EXPLANATION. (Because the presentation is given in different steps, the explanation is worked out simultaneously.) Let us draw two pictures that show this: 1. an electric mixer (T); to turn it on when there is nothing inside, when it is empty, is meaningless and worthless.

1. Living with God

God wants us to listen to him, to think of him gladly, and to pray fervently.

Daily prayers

begin with God — end with God

**Bless us, O Lord,
and these thy gifts . . .**

without fervor   fervently

Is there a way of talking like this, of talking with the mouth only, so that words come out, but words in which there are no thoughts? Such talk is empty talk. You can't talk like this to me right now because I am looking straight at you. If you talk to me, you say something *to me*. Your words will not be empty.

But when you talk with God you don't see him. That is why we must think of God, imagine him to ourselves, if we want to tell him something. This is not easy, it takes effort. And that is why we sometimes talk to God without thinking of him at all. We do not really speak to him; we say words, but we don't say them *to him*. This is like turning on an empty mixer, it is an "empty-mixer-prayer", and quite meaningless and worthless. It is a prayer without fervor, because there are no thoughts in it (T).

What would be the right way of praying? To pray means to talk with God, to say something to him. To do this we must first of all think of him, imagine him to ourselves as he really is: on his throne in heaven. Next, we must think of the words which we are saying: "Our Father . . . thy kingdom come . . . forgive us our trespasses . . . ". If we think of the words, we won't be able to say them very quickly, because it is impossible to think so quickly; we need time to think. And now our prayer becomes fervent, full of fervor. Do you know to what we can compare it? All of you have seen the censer in church. Grains of incense are placed on the burning coals, dissolve in the heat, and send a white fragrance up to heaven (draw the clouds of incense). In the same way, a fervent prayer rises up to heaven. Such a prayer is an "incense-prayer".

2. Because it is not easy to pray fervently, we need something to help us, we need a rule. It is called: morning – noon – night: "Daily Prayers" (T). In the morning when we wake up we greet mother – and if we live with God, we greet him too. The picture with the rising sun is called "morning prayer". In the evening, when we go to bed, we talk with God again. The picture with the moon in it is called "evening prayer". "Begin with God – end with God" (T). And at noon? The picture with the food on the table is called "grace at meals". In some families everyone prays

22

together. If your family does not pray, then this is what you can do: look at your plate and stir the soup as if it were too hot; and as you do this think of God, who gives us our food, and pray: "Bless us, O Lord . . ." (T).

APPLICATION. Now you understand what signpost No. 1 tells us: Living with God. Praying in the right way is part of this.

Let us close our eyes and put our hands in front of our face. We won't look outside, but inside. Did you follow the direction in which the signpost points? Did you say your evening prayers last night? And this morning your morning prayers? Fervently, or without fervor? If you did not follow the signpost say so quietly to God, in a short sentence, e.g.: "I didn't feel like praying last night." "This morning I prayed without thinking." (Some moments of silence for reflection.) God would have been glad if you had talked with him in the right way. Are you sorry that you didn't? Tell him so, and ask him to forgive you. He sees you right now from his throne in heaven and looks into your heart. (Silence). And promise him that you will pray fervently tonight. Tell him this in one sentence! (Silence).

NOTE. This exercise, which consists of the three acts of examination of conscience, contrition, and resolution, should be practiced with every signpost. If it is skilfully conducted, the catechist will find himself here at the core of preparing the children for confession: guidance to personal confession. At the same time he will be fostering their personal relationship with God.

23

2. THE HONOR OF GOD

AIM. Whereas the first signpost deals with our interior relationship to God, the second, "The honor of God", considers our external relationship to him as it manifests itself when we defend his honor. For children, this experience is ordinarily confined to the use of holy names.

PREPARATION. I brought along today a stone and a flower, we shall see why. Suppose I throw the stone at someone, what would this mean? The other day there was a report in the newspapers of people throwing stones at the car of a politician. The stones tell how much the people dislike him. What do you think he felt like?! But suppose that, instead, people had thrown flowers at the car – beautiful, fragrant flowers. The flowers would tell that they like him.

PRESENTATION. David hears a man curse in the street. He stands still, frightened. He remembers having heard someone say: "He who curses throws a stone against heaven." Then he thinks: "I shall throw a flower toward heaven", and he prays quietly in his heart: "Praised be Jesus Christ!"

EXPLANATION. 1. Cursing is as ugly as throwing stones. God does not defend himself. But I want to defend him, I want to stand up for his honor. Short prayers are like flowers thrown toward heaven.
2. "The honor of God" – this is signpost No. 2 (T). If someone does not honor God, or speaks ill of him, we must defend his honor.
3. Should David have defended God's honor aloud? Should he have said: "You must not do this, it is ugly, it is a sin!"? I think this would not have been the right thing to do in this case. Maybe the

2. The Honor of God

God wants us to honor all that is holy,
especially all holy names.

Cursing is the language of hell.

man would have become more angry still and would have continued to curse. Later on, when you are grown up, you can defend God's honor aloud, against other grown ups. David did quite right to pray quietly in his heart. He followed the signpost.

4. The back of the signpost tells us what things we must safeguard very specially: "God wants us to honor all that is holy, especially all holy names" (T).

5. All that is holy – that is, all that is consecrated or blessed: church, the cemetery, the rosary, priests, religious. Did you ever do something wrong here? (Silence).

6. But above all we must honor holy names. Much wrong is done here, even by children! And yet, how beautiful the holy names are! E.g.: Jesus Christ (the initials of both names) – Lord, our Lord and God (triangle). Anyone who misuses these names, either out of anger or out of carelessness, does something very wrong: he throws stones at the honor of God. Did you ever throw such stones against heaven? (Silence). If you did, then ask right away for forgiveness in your heart.

7. We speak English, the French speak French, in China people speak Chinese – and in hell? "Cursing is the language of hell" (T). If you hear another boy or girl use this language, say right away, "Be quiet!" This language must not be spoken among us.

APPLICATION. Which of you will make the resolution: If someone throws stones against heaven by cursing, I will right away throw a flower after them, by praying in my heart: "Praised be Jesus Christ!" or, "Holy God, we praise your name!" This can become a real habit with us. I shall ask you the next time if, when you heard someone curse, you threw a flower toward heaven to make up for it.

3. SUNDAYS AND HOLY DAYS

AIM. Going to church on Sunday is singled out from the wider obligation to keep holy the Lord's Day, and is explained.

PREPARATION. Look at the door of our classroom. If you are standing outside you cannot tell what goes on inside. But if you open the door and look in? Sometimes there is such a closed door at home – maybe the door leading into the living room on Christmas morning – we look at it with great curiosity. At long last it opens and you can look inside. ... There is another door which is more important still: the door to church. (Diagram. Draw if possible the door of the local parish church.)

PRESENTATION. Sometimes the door of an old church is beautifully decorated, so that we can tell right away how important it is. On the other side of it there is something like another world. And when it opens we look into a radiance, a glow. That is why someone once said that the door to church is almost like the door to heaven. To open it is a little like looking into heaven.

EXPLANATION. 1. When you go to our church next Sunday I want you to look carefully at the door. Now it opens, and you can look into the church – into this beautiful, holy space with lights and candles, with flowers – the altar – God lives there, as he does in heaven. Only we cannot see him.

Other people don't believe this, but we know that when we come to Mass we are God's guests – just as in heaven, only we cannot see it.

2. God invites us each Sunday and holy day, he wants us to come to church. This is signpost No. 3. We shall now write on the board what is written on both sides of this signpost (T).

3. But what if someone does not come to church? If he is sick, it

is not his fault; if he forgets, it is more serious; if he does not care, does not want to come any more, prefers to stay in bed or to do something else, like going for a ride or playing baseball – then the road of his life goes in the wrong direction. He is in danger and needs a serious warning. Listen to these words:

> He who does not find the door to church on Sunday
> will not find the door to heaven when he dies (T).

But this would be terrible! Perhaps you know people who no longer go to church – are they in danger? "Jesus, please help them to find the door to church once more and to come to Mass!" (Silence).

APPLICATION. The door to church separates what is inside from what is outside. Let us think about each.

Outside: We get there on time, we bring our missal with us. We leave talking and noise outside.

Inside: We go to our seat – how are we supposed to behave during Mass? What is the right way and what is the wrong way? Close your eyes and think of last Sunday: outside the door – now you enter – now you are in your seat – how did you behave, right or wrong? (The catechist should describe the local details, so that the children can experience their own situation. In this way he helps to prepare them for confession.)

3. Sundays and Holy Days

God wants us to participate fervently
in the Mass on Sundays and holy days.

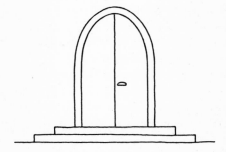

He who does not find
the door to church on Sunday
will not find the door to heaven when he dies.

4. PARENTS

AIM. To show the children what should be their relationship to their parents, by explaining to them the purpose of education.

PREPARATION. On the front of signpost No. 4 is written: "4. Parents." What is written on the back – something difficult? Let us see.

PRESENTATION. Let us draw a family. Frank, how many children are you at home? Four. Now tell me the children's names. There are four of you: Jack – Mary – Frank – Jane. This is your family. Something is still missing? These two wedding rings stand for your parents. When your parents received their wedding rings they were blessed by God, as a sign that parents undertake a sacred task for their children (diagram: the symbol for God with rays). There are lines running from God to your parents and to their children. This means something special.

EXPLANATION. 1. God gave your parents the task to look after you. We call this task "education". Is it difficult or easy? Find out by reading your parents' faces.

2. But there is a line which runs from God, through your parents, to you. What this means is written on the back of the fourth signpost: "God wants us to obey our parents and to give them joy" (T). This sounds both difficult and beautiful at the same time.

3. To obey: this means first of all that we must listen to what father and mother tell us. Some children don't listen at all when their parents speak to them. They never stop to think whether it is a good thing that their parents tell them what to do, tell them what they want of them. These children do not understand the meaning of "education".

4. I shall now draw two trees. They look quite different, yet they

30

4. Parents

God wants us to obey our parents
and to give them joy.

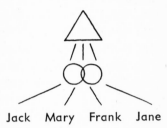

Jack   Mary   Frank   Jane

I will obey
gladly — quickly — exactly
at home — at play — at work

The educator is a gardener.

are the same age. One is small and crooked, and has only one sour apple as fruit. The other is tall and straight, it grew properly and has many apples – but it is tied to a pole. Why? Is not the first tree much better off because it could grow as it pleased? But it turned out to be no good. It needed a gardener, who would have tied

31

it to a pole and pruned its branches with shears. You can all see how necessary a gardener is.

This is just what our parents do when they educate us. They want you to grow up straight, so that one day you will be like the tall apple tree. "The educator is a gardener" (T).

5. Maybe you want at all costs to grow up crooked, since you don't listen and obey! Do you see now how foolish this is? And do you understand why "God wants us to . . ."?

6. You should help your gardeners – by obeying gladly, quickly and exactly (T). For instance, at home (the catechist briefly describes a typical situation: getting up, dressing, washing, cleaning one's teeth); at play (stopping in time to come to dinner); at work (first homework, playing comes afterwards – helping mother in the kitchen).

7. Those among you who are clever will be able to tell what your parents would like you to do. You won't wait until they ask you to do it, but you will do it of your own accord. You won't manage this always, but sometimes you will. Do you know how this makes your parents feel? It is a great joy for them. They are as pleased as the gardener is when his tree begins to bloom.

APPLICATION. The fourth signpost is very important for children. I want you today, at home, to take a look at the wedding rings of father and mother, and to think of the line which runs from God, through the rings, to you.

And now we shall again close our eyes and look inside ourselves. Are your parents your gardeners? In what ways do you make them happy? In what ways do you give them a hard time when they try to educate you?

5. NEIGHBOR

I

AIM. Because of its importance the subject of "neighbor" will be dealt with in two lessons, from a negative and from a positive point of view: what we should not do – what we should do. The first lesson explains the golden rule: "Do unto others. . . ".

PREPARATION. Which signposts are the most important ones? The first and the fifth. Let us write on the board what is written on signpost No. 5: "5. Neighbor." "God wants us to . . ." (T). The last words are, ". . . and to do him no harm." Now let us try to understand what this means.

PRESENTATION. Today we are going to pretend that we are watching a play. Instead of going into the playground with the others during the lunch break, we shall look from our windows into the yard where the other children are playing. What would we see and hear? Shouting and noise – this is healthy, because you can't sit still in your classroom all morning long. What else? The children are eating their lunch. What else? Quarrelling. Let us watch carefully. Over there one of the boys is mean and cowardly, he has just knocked down a smaller boy. And now the break is over and all the children go toward the school entrance. Most of them walk in order and quietly, but some are pushing others roughly aside in order to get ahead of them, they step on their feet and kick them. (Diagram. The right half of the diagram will be filled in only in the next class.)

EXPLANATION. 1. This was like a play. What happens in the playground at school often happens in real life.

2. Most people lead quiet and orderly lives. But there are always some who have no consideration for others, and who do them

harm. If we point this out to them and reproach them they will laugh at us. Such people deserve to be punished. But there are others who realize that they have done something wrong only when it is pointed out to them. These people need a rule:

Do unto others
as you would have others do unto you.

If someone is mean to you, you are angry. That is just what you yourself must not do to another. This rule is very precious, therefore it is called the "golden rule" (T).

APPLICATION. Now let us once again pretend to be watching, silently. Close your eyes. Let us imagine that we are looking out through the windows at ourselves in the playground. Look at yourself, what were you like yesterday? Did you obey the golden rule or not? Think for a moment what it would be like out there if suddenly everyone would obey the golden rule. What would be different? Would things be nicer in the playground? Keep your eyes closed.

We shall now switch to the street, at 5 p.m. during the rush hour. Do people obey the golden rule? Sometimes we human beings are very mean, and this causes much unhappiness. The golden rule would save us a great deal of misery.

II

AIM. Stressing the positive obligation to help others.

PREPARATION. "To do no harm to another" is only half of what is written on the back of signpost No. 5. The more beautiful half says: "To help him." (In reviewing the last class the first part of the diagram should be drawn again, and completed during the second class.)

34

5. Neighbor

God wants us to love our neighbor
as ourselves, to help him,
and to do him no harm.

The golden
rule

Do unto others as
you would have
them do unto you.

What you did to
one of these least of
my brethren, you
did it to me.

The great commandment of love!

PRESENTATION. When we walk along the street we occasionally meet someone we know; but most of the people are strangers. We know nothing about them, we have never seen them before, and probably will never see them again. Mother has warned you to be very careful with strangers. But there is one exception to this. A woman you do not know slips, falls down, and spills the contents of her bag on the road. She gets up trembling and with difficulty; she cannot bend down to pick up her things. Should you, in this case, still be careful and continue on your way?

This is the exception. The woman is in need, and "God wants us to love our neighbor as ourselves and to help him". You bend down and pick up the things the woman has dropped. In this way you are helping her.

EXPLANATION. 1. If you see a stranger in need and are able to help, then he is no longer a stranger; he is now called "neighbor".

2. If someone passes by his neighbor and does not help him, he sins against the fifth signpost – the most important signpost next to the first. Whoever sins against it does something very wrong. He sins against love, against the "great commandment of love" (T). Did this ever happen to you? (Silence).

3. Some of you look at me as though you were afraid. The other day someone asked me, "Why is this so serious, what business is it of mine? I don't even know him!" This person should carefully read what is written on the signpost: "God wants us to. . . ." In case of need, there is no longer any difference between someone we know and someone we don't know. God wants us to help both of them, e.g., that we give them to eat and drink if they are hungry (diagram: bread and cup).

4. Jesus added something quite unexpected to this great commandment of love: "What you did to one of these least of my brethren, you did it to me" (T). Whatever you do for a stranger, however poor and unimportant he may be, it is as though you had done it for Jesus. If you were to meet Jesus you would surely help him. In

36

the same way we should help all who are in need. Or would you refuse to help Jesus? From this you see that the great commandment of love is very dear to the heart of Jesus.

APPLICATION. There is one more thing I want to tell you, it is rather strange. Some people who have very good eyesight are blind if a man next to them is in need. They are blind to another's need. It is as though they were asleep, snoring loudly. We should wake such people up. "Don't you see that he is hungry, in pain, that he can't help himself, that he is sad and in need of help? Wake up, you sleepyhead!" Think how many times you pass by the fifth signpost without noticing it, and yet you encounter it almost every day. Are *you* awake, or are you too still asleep?

6. MODESTY – CHASTITY

INTRODUCTION. The subject matter of this lesson is less difficult for the children than for the catechist, for it requires thoughtful preparation on his part, including a certain amount of carefully planned verbal formulation. The lesson will have succeeded if the atmosphere in which it was held did not differ from that of other classes. The catechist should be aware of the fact that he touches here a sphere which surrounds the innermost center of the person. Whether or not the person will attain maturity depends to a large extent on the way in which sexual life and love-life were treated officially for the first time. Teaching the sacrament of penance lays foundations which can be changed only with difficulty at a later date.

AIM. The two concepts (modesty and chastity) are first of all distinguished, and the meaning of modesty is explained in terms relevant to children of eight or nine. Clear and simple concepts are what will help them most.

PREPARATION. Let us first of all write down the words written on the front and the back of signpost No. 6 (T). Modesty – to be modest. The opposite is immodesty – to be immodest.

PRESENTATION AND EXPLANATION. 1. Who knows the sixth commandment which God gave on Mount Sinai? (Maybe you look it up in your catechism): Thou shalt not commit adultery. What does this mean? A husband leaves his wife and marries another woman. This is adultery. Can you do such a thing? No, you are still too little. Here is something we must remember: chastity and adultery apply to grown ups. Before you leave school you will learn more about this; it is already now written on the signpost so that, when you grow up, you will find the right way.

2. Modesty and purity, to be modest and pure – this applies to children too. Here are some examples:

a. You are all looking forward to the summer when you can go swimming again. Where do you go? What do you take along? Bathing trunks or a bathing suit. It happened to me last year that I saw some boys hiding behind a bush and taking off their bathing trunks, and they laughed in a nasty way. That was immodest. Now we can write the sentence on the board: "He is immodest who . . ." undresses himself. There is another word for this = "uncover". We won't fill in the dots just yet, but they are important!

b. John is sick and must go to the doctor. "Get undressed." "No." "Why not?" "I may not uncover myself."

Is John right? No, because the doctor cannot examine and heal him unless he gets undressed. Why, then, is this right at the

6. Modesty and Chastity

God wants us to be modest and pure.

He is immodest who
with a bad intention

uncovers
looks at
touches
talks about

The seducer is like a rotten apple.

doctor's, if it was wrong in the case of the boys I told you about?
Because the intention is quite different: to examine and heal is
necessary and good. But the boys acted with a bad intention. Now
I shall fill in the dots on the board, "with a bad intention", and

I shall underline them in red because they are so important. Now read, please, the whole sentence: "He is immodest who, *with a bad intention*, uncovers himself."

c. Let me see if you have understood. Mother tells Jim: "Go and take your bath!" But Jim does not dare to wash himself properly. Is he right? Is he permitted to touch himself? This again depends on the intention. To wash oneself is a good intention; the boys behind the bush had a bad intention. I shall now write underneath "uncover" the word "touch".

d. Louise has a new baby brother. Mother is getting dinner ready and asks Louise to bathe her little brother. Louise keeps looking away as she does so. Mother: "Look at what you are doing, you are getting his head into the water!" But Louise is afraid to look, because her baby brother is different. Is she permitted to look at him? Yes, because she is supposed to bathe him = good intention. But what if someone looks with a bad intention, like the boys behind the bush? (T: underneath "touch", the word "look at".)

e. Suppose that after school today, on your way home, two boys talk together about what we have learned and laugh in a nasty way. This is a bad intention (T: "talk about"). I don't want you after school to discuss among yourselves what I told you. But I had to tell you about it – was this a good intention? Yes, we must talk about it because you must learn it. To learn = necessary = good intention.

f. Let us read aloud what I have written on the board. Once again, but now quietly – only the words underlined in red aloud. Why? Because they are very important. I want you to learn this sentence by heart, very thoroughly, so that you will remember it all your lives.

g. Now let us try to understand two more drawings. First, a white flower on a badge. A lily. This is the badge of a child who is modest. It would be nice if there were always lilies blooming along the road of your life.

h. The second drawing is of three beautiful red, shiny apples, sitting in a row on the shelf. One day as you look at them again they have become shrunken and brown, quite rotten. Could we have prevented this? Yes, by looking at them every day and, as soon as one apple has a brown spot, removing it, so that it will not spoil the other apples. This is a comparison.

You must stay away from children who are immodest, because they easily "spoil" or seduce other children. The seducer is like a rotten apple (T). You must tell your parents or teacher about him, otherwise he will seduce other children.

APPLICATION. At the sixth signpost there stands an invisible angel with a red flag and a drum. If someone does not follow the signpost but takes the wrong direction, the angel begins to drum loudly and hoists the red flag – in alarm! Do any of you know what the red flag and the drum are? The blush in your face, and the beating of your heart. Has it been necessary to sound this alarm for you?

(In the examination of conscience which closes the class the catechist should practice as usual the children's formation of conscience; but without becoming indiscreet, with simple questions, and using the terms that have previously been explained. In this way he will help the children to formulate in simple sentences any sins they may have committed. For instance: "I talked about it with a bad intention.")

7. PROPERTY

AIM. The experience of owning something that has been obtained by one's own effort should lead to an understanding of what it means to protect property.

PREPARATION. If signpost No. 7 did not exist we would no longer have any quiet moments. The words which are written on it are important for quiet and peace among men: "7. Property. God wants us to respect property" (T). Every one of us owns something which belongs only to him, and this we call "property".

PRESENTATION. Bill worked all summer cutting lawns for other people, saving the money he earned for a bicycle. Often he would stop in front of the store and look at the bicycle in the window, thinking: "For so and so many months and weeks I won't have any free time and I'll have to work very hard, but after that the bicycle will belong to me. That will be wonderful!" At long last the moment has come, he has saved up enough money, he is able to buy the bicycle – and rides it with joy and pride. His very own, hard-earned property!

The next day he goes shopping for his mother, and while he is in the store his bicycle is stolen. He stands there in despair, looking at the empty spot where his bicycle had stood. He cannot believe it: someone has taken *his* property! He recalls the whole long summer of hard work, and now someone has taken his bicycle, someone who had no right to it. How can anyone be so mean! He feels a dreadful anger rising in him against the thief, he deserves to be punished terribly! Pale with fury he goes to the police and reports the theft. Three days later the bicycle is returned to him, the police have caught the thief, he will be punished. But

7. Property

God wants us to respect property.

stealing-damaging
not returning borrowed goods
keeping lost property

RESTITUTION

unfortunately the bicycle already has a dent in it. Ever since that time Bill is afraid to lose what belongs to him.

EXPLANATION. 1. What has Bill learned from this experience? That the seventh signpost is very important. He has made up his mind always to distinguish very carefully between what belongs to him and what belongs to another. He will never touch another's property, not even small things, e.g., a pencil, an apple, money (diagram).

2. He has also learned to appreciate his own property better. He knows how long his father has to work in order to buy him a new suit. He is very careful with his school books, and with all the other things in school and at home. He has learned the value of money, and that there is much hard work behind it.

3. There are certain words which he now takes very seriously: stealing – damaging – not returning borrowed goods (T).

4. Bill also remembers what it feels like to lose something, how much it hurts when one's property is gone. Therefore he tells himself: "If I find something that doesn't belong to me I won't keep it (T), but will try to find the owner – by reporting it in class, or to the police."

5. There is one other thing we must think about. Suppose someone has stolen something – a candy bar – and can't return it because he has already eaten it. What now? Make up for it! He must save money, buy another candy bar, and put it on the desk of the boy whose candy bar he had taken. This is called "restitution" (T).

APPLICATION. Let us see when we are in danger of doing something wrong against the seventh signpost. If we are hungry – envious – always want to have the latest things. If my parents are not able to afford it, am I willing to go without it, or am I dissatisfied? – Do you think that property is the highest good in the world? Make a list of what belongs to you alone – to your brothers and sisters – to your parents – to your friend in school.

8. TRUTH

AIM. To bring about a living and conscious awareness of what it means to be truthful.

PREPARATION. Last time we learned about the value of property. Is truth even more precious?

Sometimes we could make something our property by lying: "Yes, this belongs to me." It takes only a few words. But? On signpost No. 8 the following words are clearly written: "8. Truth. God wants us always to speak the truth" (T).

PRESENTATION. Sometimes we enter a room in which we have difficulty breathing, because the air is stale and stuffy. We make haste to get out into fresh, clean air and take a deep breath. Sometimes the air is poisoned by something else: by untruthfulness, by lying. Our soul cannot breathe in this air. God does not want to be there. In his presence there is only clean, pure and shining truth. Christ is himself the truth (T, with the Christ-symbol and golden rays). But the devil! He likes air which is poisoned, he cannot stand the truth. He is the "father of lies" (T).

EXPLANATION. 1. To which side do you want to belong: to the followers of Christ, or to the gang of the devil? You must decide whether you want to be truthful – in your heart – in your thoughts – in your speech; or whether you are willing to lie. You must choose between the two, between Christ and the devil!

2. Let us take a good look at someone who lies. He knows the truth quite well, but he says something different. He is divided, as if his tongue were slit, like the tongue of a serpent. Lies are like a serpent winding itself around the heart (D). Once we know that someone always lies we no longer want to be near him, because the air around him is full of poison.

3. But it can be dangerous to tell the truth. If I deny that I broke the window nothing will happen to me; if I admit it I shall be punished. What am I to do? Tell the truth or lie? The devil or Christ? It takes courage to tell the truth in such a situation. "He is courageous who tells the truth even when it is dangerous" (T).

4. Some people lose all their property because they will not let go of Christ, the greatest truth of all. They need only say, "I will leave Christ, I will no longer be a Christian", and they would be able to keep all they own. But truth means more to them than their most precious possession.

APPLICATION. Let us again look into our heart. Close your eyes. Do you care whether or not you tell the truth? Think what lying does to your heart! What is the air in your classroom like? Is it truthful and clean, or poisoned by lies? Will you help to make it cleaner?

What is the air among your friends like? Do you take pride in cheating, or are you fair among each other?

What is the air at home like? Is there clean, fresh air between you and your parents, between you and your brothers and sisters?

8. Truth

God wants us to be always truthful.

Jesus Christ is truth

The devil is the father of lies

He is courageous who tells the truth
even when it is dangerous.

9. SCHOOL AND WORK

INTRODUCTION. The ninth signpost deals with an important sphere in the children's lives – with school. Ordinarily, if it is treated together with No. 4 it does not receive its due. The children should come to understand the purpose of school as preparation for life, and should realize that they will one day take up a job or profession in order to earn money, so that they can take care of themselves and of others. (Discuss briefly the various kinds of work suggested by the children.) It is important to see school in the light of a great goal given us by God, since this will provide the motivation to work hard and to obey. Later, when they are ready to leave school and to take up a job, point No. 9 should be broadened to "profession", thus focusing attention on a subject which is often neglected in the examination of conscience.

AIM. School as preparation for a job or profession (work); this should lead to the proper attitude toward school.

PREPARATION. Signpost No. 9 is strange. It is made up of two words, of which the first is valid for a time only, but the second all our life: "9. School and Work" (T). School lasts 8 years – or 12 years – sometimes 16 years or more – but its effects last all our life.

PRESENTATION. All of you have seen a house being built, maybe even a skyscraper. You remember how deep the excavations for the foundations were, and how strong and solid the foundations themselves. If the workmen don't use enough cement, the concrete will not be strong enough to support the building. The taller the building, the more solid must be the foundations. Once it is completed we no longer see the foundations; and yet the whole structure rests on them.

48

9. School and Work

God wants us to learn and to work hard.

Foundations — School

EXPLANATION. 1. All of us are engaged in building a house as long as we live – our "life-house". You have been building it already for some years – two or three of these in school. What a lot of hard work, you will think! How tall do you want your

49

house to be? Some people want to build a skyscraper, others are quite satisfied with a bungalow, some build only a cottage (T).

2. Where are the foundations for your life-house laid? In school. Later you will perhaps no longer think of school and forget all about your years there – but the solid foundations for your life-house were laid then (T).

3. There are strong foundations and there are weak ones, some go deep down, others deeper still – depending on how well we co-operate in school. One boy works hard, another is lazy; a third pays little attention; the one next to him thinks only of annoying the teacher; another reads extra books at home in his free time, in addition to his regular assignments. All this makes for different kinds of foundations, and the life-house of each will look quite different: low, tall, very tall. It is difficult to lay new foundations later and to make up for what we did not do in school. So you see that you will feel later in life the effects of what you were like in school.

4. Is God interested in the way in which we build our foundations? He has given us talents and capacities for building our life-house. How are we using them? The signpost tells us what God expects of us: "God wants us to learn and to work hard" (T). He would like us to build "beautiful houses".

5. If you want to build a *Christian* house your foundations must be extra strong, because many people will look at it critically and try to find the weak spots. Besides, it will have to stand up against many storms, and unless the foundations are strong the whole house will tumble down, i.e., the foundations of your life will be in danger. Religious instruction in school lays solid and deep foundations. Are you doing your best to help with the building?

6. We are not able to "build" alone, we need people to help us –

our teachers. Your teacher has "authority" over you, just as your boss will have in your job later on. That is why such people are called "those in authority". Sometimes we think of our teacher as if he were an enemy. But if the house is to be well built there must be order and discipline during the building operations. All of you know this very well! Why, then, do you often make life so difficult for your teacher?

APPLICATION. You have been building for some years already. Have you laid good foundations so far, or poor ones? Where are the weak spots? Where will you make a change during this week? In what way do you think of your teacher? Talk about all this now in your heart with God.

10. SELF-CONTROL

INTRODUCTION. Point 10, "Self-control", like the previous point is not only intended as an example for a page of the workbook, but also for the badly needed revision of the examination of conscience. As a rule, this point deals with those capital sins which affect one's self-education. If we explain the concept "helping in my education through self-control" to the children, they will see the capital sins not only in a negative light, but overcoming them will appear as a positive challenge. In their examination of conscience the children should clearly recognize their faults, so that they will be able to formulate the accusation.

AIM. Coming to understand and practice self-control ("mastering oneself") through the comparison of horse and rider.

PREPARATION. The last of the signposts does not stand at the end of the road of our life, but is important all our life long. It presents a challenge for adults *and* for children: "10. Self-control."

"Self-control" – "mastering oneself": what does the noun "master" mean? One who commands and gives orders, which another must obey. Are there two different people in us? Often we want to do the right thing, but our body is tired and lazy; or we are in a bad mood, and our will is helpless. It is as though we were "split", as though there were two people in us. Just like a horse which will not obey its rider.

PRESENTATION. We can learn something from the rider. Sometimes his horse is wild and strong, but it obeys him nevertheless. How is this possible? He draws in the reins almost imperceptibly, he has spurs on his boots which have sharp points and hurt (D., children enjoy drawing a horse and rider). He must practice for a long time before he has his horse completely under control. But from that time on it obeys him and is of use to him.

EXPLANATION. 1. In the same way, there is a rider and horse inside me. Who is the rider? I myself, my desire to do the right thing, my understanding. And the horse? Also I myself – my body, my talents, my faults, my weak points. These often rebel and will not obey. We need reins and spurs against ourselves, just like the rider – until we are able to master ourselves – control ourselves. "God wants us to control ourselves and to overcome our faults" (T).

2. How can we do this? Mother calls: "Time to get up!" But Ben is afraid of getting out of his warm bed, and mother has to call him three times. His body controls *him,* whereas he should control it. He needs spurs: "I *will* bear the cold", and he forces his body. Now the rider is in control of the horse.

Or: Jane is always offended if she loses at a game. She does not

52

10. Self-control

God wants us to control ourselves
and to overcome our faults.

touchy — losing one's temper
stingy — immoderate — arrogant — envious
quarrelsome

control herself, makes a long face, wants to go away. But now she
pulls in the reins and tells herself: "Come on, be brave and start
all over the next time!" She learns to master herself.

Or: Dick is strong, but he easily loses his temper and fights like a wild man. This has had some disastrous consequences! All his mother can do is to say: "Don't do this – control yourself!", but at the time when it happens she is not there. Dick buys himself a special "pair of reins": "Whenever I feel the blood mounting to my head and want to fight like a tiger, I shall first count to ten. Only after that shall I fight!" He pulls in the reins of his "inner horse" until he has practiced it many times. This is difficult. But he notices that by the time he has finished counting his anger has become less violent, and he is able to think more calmly. The rider is again in command of his horse.

Or: Anne takes great care of her clothes and toys and of all that belongs to her. But she is so attached to her things that she never wants to share anything with others, she wants to have it all to herself. This is how one becomes a miser! So she forces herself to share her lunch at school, and she even gives one of her toys to another girl. It is hard, she must give her horse the spurs and force him, like the rider. But for nothing in the world does she want to become a miser! She masters her tendency to be stingy and overcomes her fault. (Give further examples of being immoderate – arrogant – envious – quarrelsome – touchy. T.)

APPLICATION. Who knows some famous saints who rode on horseback? St. Martin of Tours, St. George. Did these men achieve self-control? Find a picture of one of them and put it above your bed. Look up at it once a day and ask yourself: "When was my horse stronger than I, and when did I master my horse?" Let us do this right now. Close your eyes and look into yourself. How did you get out of bed this morning? How will you do it to-morrow?

AIM. After each of the ten signposts has been explained separately, they are taken together as a whole, and the way in which they differ from the ten commandments is pointed out. This is followed by an examination of conscience.

PREPARATION. With our eyes we can look out into the wide world; if we close our eyes we can still see the world, by imagining it to ourselves. With closed eyes we can see something else too – our heart. But for this we need a special kind of "mirror", which we call "examination of conscience" (T).

PRESENTATION. If we look into a mirror made of glass we need light (diagram: mirror and rays of light); if it is dark outside, we can no longer see anything in the mirror.

But if we want to look into this special kind of "mirror" we do not need light from the outside. We close our eyes; but now we need another kind of light, the Holy Spirit. He enlightens my mind, so that I can see into my heart and can tell where there is good and where there is evil in it, so that I can discover my sins.

EXPLANATION. 1. This "mirror" consists of 10 signposts. We shall list them once again, all together (T). These are not the 10 commandments; we call them "10 signposts" or, from now on, "10 points". The 10 commandments of Mount Sinai are contained in the first 8 points; but they are not enough, that is why the 10 points tell us still more about what Christ wants of us.

2. The Holy Spirit will let his light shine in us if we ask him to. Therefore we must pray each time before looking into our mirror: "Come, Holy Spirit, enlighten me, so that I can see my sins" (T).

3. Going about this in the right way and looking into the mirror

courageously and honestly is called "examination of conscience". So far we have done it with each signpost separately; from now on you are do it for all ten.

APPLICATION. Now we shall practice this. Let us close our eyes and ask the Holy Spirit to enlighten us. I shall pray the words first: "Come, Holy Spirit. . . ." Now repeat them, but each one quietly in his own heart. Now let us look into the mirror. (The catechist speaks slowly.) 1. Living with God. God wants us to listen to him, to think of him gladly, and to pray fervently. What about you? . . . When did you last talk with God and pray to him? Perhaps one of you must say: "I forgot all about God, I have not prayed for several days." . . . Think how it is with you . . . But perhaps all is well, and you have nothing to say. Then remember for your confession: "1. Living with God – nothing."

(All the 10 points are reviewed in this way. Then the catechist guides the children to ask God for forgiveness and to promise to do better in the future. The children are given the task to repeat this at night before going to sleep. The catechist should continue to practice the examination of conscience with them until they gradually become used to doing it on their own. This practice is also recommended for later years from time to time, since it makes possible the adaptation of the examination of conscience to the experiences of the children as they grow older.)

Examination of Conscience

Come, Holy Spirit, enlighten me,
so that I may see my sins!

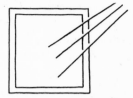

1. Living with God
2. The honor of God
3. Sundays and holy days
4. Parents
5. Neighbor
6. Modesty and chastity
7. Property
8. Truth
9. School and work
10. Self-control

CONTRITION

INTRODUCTION. Contrition is taught in two sections: asking forgiveness of God the Father – in this case, out of fear (imperfect contrition) – and asking forgiveness of Jesus – out of love (perfect contrition). As the religious education of the children is continued, the prayers of contrition should of course be broadened so as to awaken perfect contrition also towards the Father. This is part of the task of religious instruction in the upper grades. The children must also be encouraged to ask for forgiveness in their own words. But the value of having learned thoroughly a few prayer formulas has proved itself time and again, both in teaching contrition in general, and as a help for those children who are not yet able to pray in their own words.

AIM. The first lesson on contrition places God the Father into the center, in the figure of judge. The assuming of the punishment by Christ already makes the transition into the mystery of the sacrament of penance.

PREPARATION. Do you remember our first lesson on confession, the one on the confessional as judgment seat? In order to receive the sacrament we must climb up five steps. Who can name them? "1. Examination of conscience . . ." We have already practised this first step, with the "mirror". Now comes the second step, contrition (T). Contrition – to be contrite – that is to say, "I am sorry, I ask for forgiveness". How do we do this in the right way?

PRESENTATION. Let us draw a pair of scales. On one side we shall place an apple – the other side of the scales is high up in the air. And now a second pair of scales – someone has placed a drop of blood on the empty side. This drop weighs more than the apple. What is the meaning of this?

58

Contrition

Dear Father in heaven! I have
deserved a just punishment . . . .

Forgive me my sins!

Your mercy and the blood of
Jesus take away our sins.

EXPLANATION. 1. The apple stands for sin, since it was the cause of the first sin. This means that, when we go to confession, after we have examined our conscience we place our sins on one side of the scales. Are they heavy? Although the 10 signposts tell us

59

quite clearly what God *wants* of us, we have not done it, we have disobeyed. Can this have little weight?

2. What does God the Father think of it? Is he more angry with us than our father and mother? Do you realize that God knows much better even than our parents how much evil and misery come from sin? We may not appear before him with our scales weighted so heavily on one side. First, my punishment must be placed on the other side, so that my disobedience is paid for. What if God were to punish me right then for my sins?

3. What are we to do? Now listen carefully to a great, difficult, and beautiful secret! If we ask God the Father to forgive us – "Dear Father in heaven, I have deserved a just punishment" (think of the scales), "please forgive me my sins" (T) – if we ask this a second and a third time, something happens:

4. Jesus Christ places a drop of his blood on the other side of the scales, and the Father forgives. Merciful judgment is given: "Your mercy and the blood of Jesus take away our sins" (T). Should we not thank God the Father afterwards with all our heart for forgiving us?

5. How much pain did this drop of blood cost Jesus when he shed his blood for us on the cross! Now we are able to understand how the sacrifice of the cross is related to confession. On the cross, Jesus took the punishment for our sins upon himself and made up for them – and ever since he places a drop of his blood on the other side of the scales. That is why we should thank Jesus with all our heart for these drops of his blood!

6. If someone does not want to come to this court where merciful judgment is given he will find himself after his death standing with his scales before God – but now it is too late to be sorry. His punishment will be placed relentlessly on the other side of the scales!

APPLICATION. Contrition is the second and most important of all the five steps. If someone goes to confession and omits this step, his confession is worthless. He is like a man who sets about cleaning his room with only the broom stick in his hand. If you remember this comparison you will never enter the confessional poorly prepared.

DEAREST JESUS

AIM. A prayer of contrition to Jesus as example of perfect contrition.

PREPARATION. In contrition we should not think only of God the Father but also of Jesus, who paid for our sins on the cross. "Lamb of God, who takest away the sins of the world" – this is how we pray to him. It was also my sins that caused him pain.

PRESENTATION. Either a good picture of Christ on the cross, or the whole diagram at once: crown of thorns – spear and sponge – nails.

EXPLANATION. If we were able to talk with Jesus on the cross and ask him: "Dearest Jesus! Why do you wear the painful crown of thorns?" (T), which hurt your head so much, we ourselves must give the answer: "I know it is my fault too, I have been thinking so many bad things." (To help the children remember, point out the parallel: crown of thorns – head – thinking.)

"Dearest Jesus! Why do you thirst and drink vinegar and gall?" (T) "I know it is my fault too, I have been saying so many bad things" (thirst – tongue – speaking).

"Dearest Jesus! Why do sharp nails pierce your hands and feet?" (T) "I know it is my fault too, I have been doing so many bad things."

"Dearest Jesus! I am sorry to have caused you so much pain. Forgive me, I will be better from now on!"

APPLICATION. Learn this prayer by heart. We can pray it when we see a crucifix. Whenever we go to confession let us pray it three times.

Dearest Jesus!

Why do you wear the painful crown of thorns? †

Why do you thirst and drink vinegar and gall? †

Why do sharp nails pierce your hands and feet?

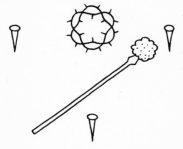

I am sorry to have caused you so much pain. Forgive me, I will be better from now on.

AIM. The resolution is seen in the light of a general promise to change and improve, but also as being within reach of the children.

PREPARATION. From a spring flows forth water – from contrition flows forth the resolution (T). The word means "to resolve", "to make a resolution" (T).

PRESENTATION. Mary asks her mother to forgive her for having come home late from school. Mother forgives, but the very next day Mary is again late. This time mother does not forgive. How can she forgive, since Mary will do it again tomorrow? Mary now realizes that she must not only ask for forgiveness, but that she must also promise something: "I won't do it again tomorrow, I will come straight home!"

EXPLANATION. 1. If today we go to confession and tomorrow we commit the same sins again, God also does not forgive us. Our contrition is not genuine unless it is accompanied by a resolution.

2. This requires two things. First, we promise God to do better from now on. Say this in a few words!

3. But this is not enough, we must also make a definite, firm resolution. David makes the resolution, "From now on I shall always obey, always!" This is a big resolution, will he be able to keep it? Better make a small one: "Today and tomorrow I shall do exactly as mother says!" So you see, our resolution should be small.

Anne promises: "This afternoon I won't quarrel with my sister." But by the time she comes home she has forgotten all about it. Her resolution was not firm. Our resolution, therefore, must be small but firm.

4. Such a small but firm resolution is like a sword. If I notice that

Resolution

to resolve — to make a resolution —
to improve

Make a small but firm resolution . . . .

I will fight the good fight!

the devil wants to tempt me to commit a sin by whispering to my heart, "Do this!", and I hold tight to my resolution, it is as though I am fighting with a sword the good fight against the serpent (diagram).

APPLICATION. Let us, for practice, think of a resolution which we want to carry out this afternoon: "Make a small but firm resolution" (T), e.g.: This afternoon . . . tonight . . . the next time I make a visit in church . . . the next time I see Joan . . . .

CONFESSION OF SINS

AIM. The confession of sins in the confessional is for many children the only occasion on which they have to speak responsibly and clearly, all on their own. Today's lesson gives a survey of what they must do in the confessional. The confession of sins according to the 10 points is "framed" between the two short prayers.
It is important to give a clear and sober explanation of the seal of confession.

PREPARATION. After the examination of conscience, after contrition and the resolution, you are ready to go into the confessional. You may now enter it and, of your own free will, accuse yourself by confessing your sins.

PRESENTATION. The penitent kneels down, quietly makes the sign of the cross, and begins in a low voice: "Bless me, Father, for I have sinned: 1. Living with God. I have . . ." etc., – all the 10 points. At the end he says: "I am heartily sorry for these and for all my sins" (T). The priest then knows that the confession of sins is finished.

EXPLANATION. 1. Let us see what sort of child would confess like this: (The catechist now gives examples of typical confessions, e.g., what a good-hearted boy, but one who is always fighting, would have to say – one who is careless and sloppy – a girl who is touchy and selfish – one who is good and devout. He formulates

Confession of Sins

Bless me, Father, for I have sinned:

1.
2.
3.
4.
5.
6.
7.
8.
9.
10.

I am heartily sorry for these
and for all my sins!

The seal of confession:
The priest is silent like a tomb.

the sentences, pausing between each so that the children have time
to think whether or not it applies to them. This provides once
again the opportunity to help them formulate their confession of
sins individually. Afterwards they are again asked to close their

eyes and to make their own confession quietly to themselves. Contrition and resolution close this practice.)

2. Who hears our confession of sins? The priest – and God hears it also. Only these two.

Think what grave sins are sometimes told! But things which people would keep strictly secret and would never tell to anyone else, they dare tell in the confessional, because they know that the priest will never betray them. Everything that is told in the confessional is kept secret, the priest never speaks about it. This is called the "seal of confession" (T). The priest is silent about it like a tomb (T – diagram). No matter how long someone would ask, or even threaten in front of a tomb, the one who lies down there will not speak. So too the priest will never speak about the sins that have been confessed (tell the story of St. Nepomuk[1]).

APPLICATION. Once the confession of sins is over, the penitent is happy. Even though it is hard to accuse ourselves, we are glad afterwards to have done it. What will God now do to us?

NOTE. There is a further way in which we can help the children to remember and practice the 10 points. In the beginning, they should always say "1., 2., 3.", etc. Even if at a given point they have nothing to confess, they should say so, e.g., "5. Neighbor – nothing." The following year, when confession is reviewed, the 10 points are written on the board. As different examples of confession are given, all those points where no accusation is necessary

---

[1] St. Nepomuk lived during the middle ages. He was confessor to the queen of Bohemia. One day the king suspected the queen of having sinned. He called St. Nepomuk and commanded him to tell him what the queen had confessed. St. Nepomuk refused, and the king used all sorts of threats. When this was of no avail, the king had him thrown from a high stone bridge into the river Moldau. Thus St. Nepomuk was martyred because he would not break the seal of confession.

are erased, so that it is now possible to say: "1. Living with God. I have . . . 4. Parents" – and the points in between are omitted. At a later stage the children should formulate only the accusation, and omit the numbers. Anyone who has prepared children for confession over several years knows that he must never demand any single step too soon. And he has also come to realize how fruitful a firm "scaffolding" for confession proves to be, and how grateful most children are for every external help we can give them.

INSIDE THE CONFESSIONAL

This lesson describes everything that happens in the confessional, and brings together all the individual details. The task of the priest is further explained: he not only remits sins, he may also ask questions on any relevant points. The priest will remember to confine himself only to what is essential. So much depends for their later life on the children's early experience of confession: either harm will be done, or they will think of the sacrament of penance as a source of grace. The priest's attitude toward his penitents should never be any other than gentleness and kindness. The *conversation* in the confessional must be explained as the right which any judge has to question, if something in the confession of sins was not clear to him, or if there is doubt as to the sincerity of the sinner. (The latter eventuality is usually taken care of in the "exhortation", which tries to call forth once again contrition at the moment of absolution.)

The imposition of a *penance* is discussed, with a view to possible difficulties that may arise: "I can't do this" – "I beg your pardon, I did not understand" – "Thank you", if everything is clear. The absolution also is explained only in its external aspect (T: a purple stole as insignia for the priestly power).

The parting greeting, "Go in peace . . ." is at the same time described as dismissal: "You may not leave before!"

The lesson follows the structure of the diagram.

Inside the Confessional

1. Confession of sins

2. The priest questions

3. The priest imposes a
   penance ("Thank you")

4. THE ABSOLUTION

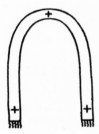

5. The parting greeting

ABSOLUTION

INTRODUCTION. Now that the technical aspects of confession have been covered, attention and time should be given to the interior happenings between God and penitent. The child must come to understand the part which the three divine Persons play during the absolution, so that, for one moment after the absolution is given, there will reign in the confessional a sacred silence. Only then does the priest give the parting greeting. This lesson is the real introduction into the mystery of the sacrament of penance.

AIM. The formula of absolution, and what happens during the mystery – represented in the three divine Persons.

PREPARATION. At every court trial there comes a moment when everyone holds his breath: when the judge is about to pronounce the verdict. Accuser and accused, all the people present in the court room, know that the decision will now be made. It is the same in confession, when the absolution is given.

PRESENTATION. All grows still in the confessional, the priest prays and raises his right hand. You can tell that at this moment he is exercising a great power. And as he raises his hand he pronounces words in Latin, words which are so important that we shall write them down both in Latin and English and shall memorize them: *Ego te absolvo a peccatis tuis* – I absolve you from your sins. In the name of the Father, and of the Son, and of the Holy Spirit (T). And as he says this he makes the sign of the cross with his hand (diagram: purple cross, with the Latin text in red underneath). Now it has happened, this was the verdict: absolution in the merciful judgment of confession.

EXPLANATION. 1. During the absolution we can see two things

Absolution

I absolve you from your sins
in the name of the Father, and of the Son,
and of the Holy Spirit. Amen.

EGO TE ABSOLVO A PECCATIS TUIS

GOD THE FATHER forgives my sins
GOD THE SON gives me his precious blood
GOD THE HOLY SPIRIT makes my heart clean

(raising of the hand and the sign of the cross), and hear one thing (the formula of absolution).

2. What we can see and hear points to something invisible that is happening. If we could see and hear like angels, we would be able

73

to see what God the Father, God the Son, and God the Holy Spirit do at this moment. For the priest says: "In the name of the Father . . ." (T: God the Father – God the Son – God the Holy Spirit).

3. At this moment God the Father forgives our sins (T: forgives sins). When the priest speaks the absolution it is as though we could hear God the Father forgive us. All that weighed upon us is now taken away, we can once again be happy, all that stood between God and myself is all right again! I will thank him later with all my heart.

At this moment God the Son places a drop of his precious blood on my scales: he pays the price, he has endured the punishment, he helps me, he is my Saviour! I will thank him later with all my heart.

At this same moment the Holy Spirit touches my heart and makes it clean again. A wonderful thing takes place in my soul! It becomes as clean as it was at the moment of baptism. I will thank the Holy Spirit later with all my heart.

APPLICATION. We don't feel any of this, but it does really happen in us, invisibly, in our souls. We don't feel it but we know it. This is the most sacred moment of confession. We would like, if possible, to hold our breath and to be completely still. Only then does the priest speak the parting greeting, and I leave the confessional and go to a pew, where I can be all by myself.

AFTER CONFESSION

INTRODUCTION. The children must be carefully prepared as to what they should do right after confession, so that their piety will from the first be firmly rooted. If a long waiting outside the confessional can be avoided they should come without their prayer books, so that they will have to rely only on what they have learned and on their own initiative.

AIM. Thanksgiving and penance are explained in the light of a change of heart.

PREPARATION. If we have escaped a great danger we heave a big sigh of relief. If someone leaves the court room after he has been set free, it will seem to him that he can breathe again. And what about you, when you leave the merciful judgment of confession? What will you do? First, you will surely heave a sigh of relief that it is over. But afterwards, when you are kneeling in the pew thinking back over what has happened? You will do two things: 1. Thanksgiving, 2. Penance (T).

PRESENTATION. Jesus once told the story of a man to whom the king forgave an enormous debt – he simply remitted it. It was as though he had given him back his life. He can start all over, full of gratitude toward his lord, he can mend his ways, he can be as good and kind toward others as his lord has been to him. And that is what the king expected of him! But – after leaving the king's presence he meets in the street someone who owes him a small sum of money. He grabs him by the shoulder, shakes him, and demands his money right there and then (cf. Matt. 18:23 ff.).

EXPLANATION. 1. What about this man? He has not changed a bit, he has not become better, he is not grateful at all. This is what we are like if we hurry out of church right away and carry on exactly as we did before. Every time we go to confession there is a new beginning. *I* have become different, *I* have changed.

2. You kneel down in your pew, alone, cover your face with your hands and thank God. What has God done for me? Suddenly you realize that your thoughts can become prayer: "God the Father, you have forgiven me – I thank you" (three times). "God the Son, you have given me your precious blood – I thank you" (three times). "God the Holy Spirit, you have made my heart clean – I thank you" (three times).

You are able to pray like this now, independently and without a prayer book, because you have understood what happened to you in confession.

3. After the thanksgiving comes the penance. The priest told you to say a prayer, this is called the "penance". What is its meaning? It is not a punishment, but:

If your mother has forgiven you something very bad and is no longer angry with you, you want to show her that you have changed. You want to do something nice for her, help her in some way, so that she will know you have really changed, really become different. This is called "change of heart". (T. For the catechist: this word has exactly the same meaning as *metanoia*.) It is like turning around (T) on a wrong road someone has taken (diagram). He turns around interiorly, he acts differently. If he was unkind to his mother before, he now does something nice for her: this is what the penance in confession is like. But this is just what the ungrateful man of whom Jesus spoke did not do – he did not change. The prayer which we pray after confession, our penance, is a sign which is meant to show God that we have changed, that we have become different. Our penance is a sign of our change of heart.

After Confession

1. Thanksgiving
2. Penance

change of heart — turning around — penance

Confession makes us free

4. This prayer, this penance, is usually quite short. Should we do more besides, on our own? A voluntary penance? Think of one, if you like (the catechist can give some examples).

APPLICATION. After you have prayed your penance make a large

sign of the cross, genuflect reverently and slowly, and go home.
You will see that "confession makes us free" (T).

HOW OFTEN SHALL I GO TO CONFESSION?

AIM. This last lesson on the sacrament of penance lays foundations
for the future – for the remaining years in school as well as for
later life.

PREPARATION. We shall go to confession many times in our
lives: some of us will go very frequently, some more rarely, some
perhaps not at all for a long time. Many people keep putting
it off – to next month – next Saturday – tomorrow – until it
is too late. But "too late" can be a very dangerous business.

PRESENTATION. Jack has a toothache, but does not want to go to
the dentist. "Not today, tomorrow." By the end of the day the
tooth hurts so much that he can't stand it any longer. "Mother,
let's go after all, right away!" They come to the dentist's office,
but he has just left. Too late! Now he must bear the pain all
through the night, until morning. "If only – if only I had gone
earlier!"

EXPLANATION. 1. Suppose this happens with confession – too
late – because someone kept putting it off; and suddenly he dies.
In the next world he will not receive merciful judgment, but
punishment for his sins instead. Too late!

2. There is a clock (diagram) which ticks 1 – 2 – 3 (T). He who
listens to its ticking knows when it is time to go to confession and
will go while there is still time. The clock tells him how often he
should go (T – title).

3. "Must – once a year" (T). The Church says that this is the

How Often Shall I go to Confession?

1. Must: once a year
(commandment of the Church)

2. Should: whenever a sin troubles me a
great deal

3. My resolution . . . .

Each day of confession is a day of grace!

minimum, and commands it. That is why we call it "commandment of the Church" (T).

4. Should – whenever some sin is troubling me (T). Sins trouble us in different degrees, just as there are small wounds and large ones

(a pin prick, a deep cut from a knife). In the case of a large wound we go to the doctor right away, without waiting. If a sin is troubling me a great deal, then there is a large wound in my soul, and I shall not wait for a whole year, until I *must* go to confession. No, for it might be too late by that time! I shall go without absolutely having to go, on my own, and right away. If your mother is very angry with you – for one day, for two days – can you stand it? This is a dreadful thing! If a sin is troubling me a great deal it is a sign that something is very wrong between God and me: I cannot stand it any longer that he is angry with me. (For the catechist: the comparison with different kinds of wounds, i.e., venial sins, must of course be taken up again later and explained in more detail, until the distinction between venial sin and mortal sin has become clear.)

5. The clock, however, tells something else as well to children who are still in school. Although we *must* go to confession only once a year, and although we probably shall not commit a very grave sin too often, nevertheless we shall go to confession frequently: because it is good to receive merciful judgment, and because you must learn how to go to confession properly; you can learn this only by going often. So let us, while we are in school, make a resolution – "once a month" (T). Later, when you grow up and leave school, many of you will continue to make this resolution, while others will perhaps make a different resolution, e.g., to go four times a year. But all of us must always observe points 1 and 2.

APPLICATION. How many days of confession will there be in your life? Better too many than too few, better once too often than too late. And now, memorize this sentence: "Each day of confession is a day of grace" (T).

The Eucharist

The purpose of the lessons which follow is to deepen the understanding of the eucharist for children of eight or nine. This means nothing else than introducing them to participation in the Mass. These lessons are, therefore, essentially lessons on the Mass. The Mass should not, however, be explained to the children from a dogmatic viewpoint. What they need in order to learn to participate in the Mass is a genuine, though child-like introduction into the mystery of the eucharist in all its breadth and depth. Our starting point will be, therefore, not a dogmatic definition, but that which the children see: the external form of the Mass, which is a communal meal. Once this has been grasped we can proceed to the interior action.

This approach may be characterized as pastoral-theological approach, in contrast to the dogmatic approach. Beneath the veil of a meal the sacrifice is concealed; similarly, our teaching must proceed from what is outside to what is within.

THE BREAD OF THE MASS

AIM. This first, introductory lesson on the Mass provides the real starting point: contact with the glorified Lord.

PREPARATION. Do you remember the day when you received holy communion for the first time? That was a beautiful day! Since then time has passed, and you have become older, able to understand things more deeply. So we shall now begin to try and understand the mystery of holy communion more deeply.

PRESENATTION. I said that holy communion is a mystery. Not only because we do not understand how the bread is changed, but also because it contains something mysterious, just like a treasure chest which contains a treasure. If you open the chest the gold and jewels shine out so brightly that we would like to keep on looking at all this splendor and beauty.

It is the same with the mystery of holy communion. If we could see the mystery, it would shine forth brightly (diagram: ciborium with host and golden rays). From where do these rays come?

EXPLANATION. We shall find the answer if we think of other names for holy communion. Let us write them on the board: holy communion – holy bread – heavenly bread – sacred host – body of Jesus (T). Instead of "holy communion," let us say "holy bread" (title).

The most mysterious name is the last: the "body of Jesus". The holy bread is the body of Jesus! Imagine if we could see this!? Then we would see Jesus! As baby, lying in the manger? No. Wandering through the Holy Land and working miracles? No. Jesus hanging on the cross? No. All this is now past. What is Jesus like now? After the resurrection the apostles saw him with a new body, bright and shining, we say "glorified" (diagram: Christ-symbol with golden rays). This is how he is now in heaven – and in the holy bread. This is the mystery that shines in holy communion. If only we could see it!

APPLICATION. Now we understand something else too. When we eat this holy bread Jesus comes into our heart. So let us ask him to shine in our heart with his wonderful body: "Lord Jesus come, and in my heart shine forth!" It would be very good if all of you, from now on, would softly pray this prayer three times every night, before going to sleep.

The Holy Bread

holy communion — holy bread —
heavenly bread — sacred host — body of Jesus

Lord Jesus come,
and in my heart shine forth!

AIM. The two miracles of the marriage at Cana and the multiplication of the loaves can give the experience of looking up at the Lord and longing for his nearness. Understanding the concepts "to transform" and "to multiply" are secondary fruits of this lesson.

PREPARATION. What is our new communion prayer? "Lord Jesus come . . .". All those who have prayed it each evening, look at me; those who forgot to pray it, close your eyes. (This semi-public control is meant to encourage the children more intensively to practice their prayers.) Today we are going to see how it is that Jesus can "shine". Did he do this also while he was still living in the Holy Land?

PRESENTATION. People often used to look at Jesus, but there were moments when they looked at him with wonder and joy, as though they were seeing something new, as though he were radiant and shining. Let us draw two such moments (drawing of the two wine jars, and of the bread basket and fish).

EXPLANATION. a. What is the title of the first drawing? The marriage at Cana. The people were in need, there was not enough wine. What did Jesus do? He spoke softly some words over the water and blessed it (diagram: a red cross over the wine jars), and it was changed into wine. This showed the people that Jesus had the power "wonderfully to transform" (T).

How, do you think, the people now looked at Jesus? Surprised – in wonder – with love – with enthusiasm – as though it were good being near him – almost as though he were shining, in an invisible way.

b. What is the title of the second drawing? The miraculous multi-

The Lord Feeds the People of God

The Lord is my shepherd —
You prepare a table for me —
and I shall dwell
in the house of the Lord.

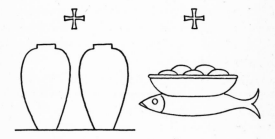

Christ has the power wonderfully
to transform and multiply.

plication of loaves. Again there was a need, the people were hungry. What did Jesus do? He spoke softly some words over the five loaves and two fishes and blessed them (diagram: the red cross), and there were enough loaves and fishes for everyone. And as all the people ate and were filled (5000 men, not counting the women and children), they saw that Jesus had the power wonderfully to "multiply" (complete the sentence on the board).

How, do you think, did the people now look at Jesus? In admiration and enthusiasm – near him there is no need – near him the entire people would live in happiness and joy – as though God himself were here at last, caring for all. As the morning star shines in the dark night, so too Jesus shines, because he has divine power. With this power he shines also in us, in holy communion.

Now let us think of a title for the entire lesson. Jesus, the Lord, feeds all who belong to him, his people, the people of God. We too belong to this people of God (T).

APPLICATION. Let us write a second prayer on the board which we can pray when we receive holy communion, a verse from a holy song (Psalm 22): "The Lord is my shepherd – you prepare a table for me – and I shall dwell in the house of the Lord" (T).

JESUS PROMISES HEAVENLY BREAD

AIM. The lesson about the promise of the eucharist can be full of dramatic tension, if the presentation has as its goal the question, "Will you also go away?" The faith of the children is challenged, because it is difficult to believe the words Jesus speaks here, and only trust in his person and word can give the courage to do so.

PREPARATION. Did the people always believe Jesus after they had seen that he had the power wonderfully to transform and to multiply? We now come to a difficult point, where men have different reactions and go their separate ways.

PRESENTATION. (Dramatic description of Jesus' discourse on the

Jesus Promises Heavenly Bread

"I am the bread of life. — My flesh is food indeed, my blood is drink indeed. — He who eats of this bread shall live forever."

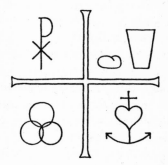

My answer: "Jesus, I believe you, I hope in you, I love you! Amen."

eucharist in simplified form; the main emphasis is on those sentences which are of special importance catechetically): "I know why you seek me – because you ate yesterday of the bread I gave you. But I have a bread for eternal life." "Give us this bread!"

"I am the bread of life." (T and diagram: first a thin, large cross, which is later filled in with strong lines and colored in red, so that it becomes a beautiful and finished symbol; a yellow Christ-symbol is drawn into the upper left-hand corner.) The people thought: How can a man who is alive be bread? Jesus did not explain, but went on: "My flesh is food indeed. My blood is drink indeed" (diagram: bread for eating – cup for drinking). The people murmured at these words, but again Jesus did not explain, but went on: "Whoever eats of this bread shall live forever" (diagram: three rings, an ancient symbol for the eternal life of the triune God).

EXPLANATION. a. What did Jesus promise? The three symbols tell us the answer: He is the bread of life – his flesh is this food – he who eats of it will live forever.

It is easy to remember this, but hard to understand it. The people who heard these words shook their heads and went away – even though the day before they had seen the miracle of the multiplication of the loaves. Because they don't understand how this can be, they don't believe him. Many people today do the same thing.

b. In the end only the apostles remained. Was Jesus afraid that they too would leave him? No, he asks them point-blank: "Will you also go away?" He wants only those to remain with him who believe him. And now Peter gives a very important answer: "Lord, to whom shall we go? You have the words of eternal life." Or, as we would say: "Lord, it is true that I don't understand this, but because you say that it is so I believe you." Not to understand, and yet to believe – because *he* says so, because we trust *him,* as a child trusts his father, as one trusts a friend.

APPLICATION. a. If Jesus were to ask *us*: "Will you also go away?", what would our reply be? "Lord, we don't understand

88

either, it is true, but we believe you!" Let us carefully write and draw this answer: "Jesus, I believe you (the blue cross in the drawing). – "I hope in you." I hope for eternal life! (the green anchor). – "I love you" (the red heart; these three figures form the symbol of the three theological virtues of faith, hope and charity).
b. Now we know already three prayers for communion time: "Lord Jesus, come" – "The Lord is my shepherd" – "Jesus, I believe you . . ." Let us pray them all every evening this week before going to sleep.

THE SACRIFICE OF THE CROSS

AIM. The next two lessons belong together. They are meant to show the body of the Lord as sacrificial gift, and in his present, glorified state.

PREPARATION. We shall see today how precious is that "holy bread" which Jesus promised us. For it cost an enormous price: his life.

PRESENTATION. (Preferably with the aid of a good picture of the crucifixion. Draw in outline the hill, the cross, the body – in its place the heart with the blood trickling down.)

EXPLANATION. Something visible and something invisible happened on the cross (T), that is to say, something happened outside, and something happened inside.

a. Visible: the people could see how his body died and his blood was shed. This cost Jesus terrible pain.

b. Invisible: in his heart Jesus thought, I will not defend myself, I *will* to do this, because I want to obey my Father in heaven: because I want to purchase eternal life for mankind. As price I am offering two gifts – my body and my blood.

c. That is why we call his body and blood the visible gifts; the invisible thoughts in his heart we call surrender. The gifts and the surrender together are called "sacrifice" (T), and because it happened on the cross it is called "the bloody sacrifice of the cross" (T — title).

APPLICATION. a. Do you realize how much the "holy bread" which Jesus gives us cost? It is very precious. Will the longing to receive it grow in you?

b. Let us look at the crucifix in our classroom. We see the visible part of the sacrifice of the cross, the sacrificial gifts. Now think of what we cannot see, the surrender in Jesus' heart. It is invisible, but still part of the cross. And because Jesus offered himself without defending himself, like a sacrificial lamb, we call him the "lamb of God". During Mass we pray: "Lamb of God, who takest away the sins of the world, have mercy on us" (T). This is a fourth prayer for communion.

The Sacrifice of the Cross

visible — gifts | SACRIFICE | price for
invisible — surrender | | eternal life

Lamb of God
who takest away the sins of the world,
have mercy on us!

AIM. To come to see the present reality of the glorified Lord as the unique and actual "state" of salvation in general, and specifically as the "Kyrios" of the Mass.

PREPARATION. To celebrate Mass is a joyful thing. But what if we were to think of Jesus on the cross at that moment? Then we would be sad, not joyful. What Jesus experienced after his sacrifice on the cross, however, is so glorious that it casts light even on the darkness of Good Friday, and from this comes the joy at Mass.

PRESENTATION. Let us look at this picture (a good picture of the risen Lord, perhaps with the disciples on the way to Emmaus. Describe what he looked like, his coming and disappearing.)

EXPLANATION. a. Jesus is risen from the dead and appears to his disciples. He has begun a new life, the disciples can see it.

b. There is no more sorrow, no more pain. The sacrifice has been made, now there only is joy and eternal life in him. That is why he is surrounded by rays in the picture. Rays of light are rays of joy and of life (T: light – joy – life).

c. His body is the same as it was before, we can see the wounds in it, they remind us of the sacrifice. But it is also changed, gloriously risen, filled with wonderful life, as though the light of joy were shining through it. We say that the body of Jesus is now glorified.

d. Since that time, nearly 2000 years have gone by. But we know that Jesus is exactly the same today, in heaven on his throne, ever since his Ascension. Since that day he is called the "Lord," we call him the "glorified Lord" (T – title and diagram: a red Christ-symbol with crown and golden rays).

APPLICATION. a. When we pray to Jesus we must think of him

Jesus the Glorified Lord

new life — joy — light

Kyrie eleison!

like this. This glorified, glorious king is *our* Lord, who cares for us and who guides the entire world toward a good ending.

b. During Mass too this is how we pray to him. We call out: Lord – look down on us – come to us – help us – have mercy on us.

In the beautiful ancient Greek language this is called: "Kyrie eleison." (T. Practice the prayer for Mass, and pray it at the end of class.)

THE LAST SUPPER

AIM. The structure of Last Supper is shown to be the basic form which underlies the Mass.

PREPARATION. Whenever we go to Mass we participate in a celebration. This celebration began on a day long ago, the first time there ever was a Mass. Already then it was the same as our Mass, only much simpler. And it was not yet called the "Mass", but the "Last Supper" (T).

PRESENTATION. (A picture of the Last Supper. While all look at it, describe what took place – the setting of the table – the prayer of Jesus – the passing of the holy food. Rather than letting the children tell the details, the catechist should give a precise and reverent account of what happened, without explanation or comments.)

EXPLANATION. Now let us draw and write down the most important things that happened. In the center stood a table (D) beautifully decorated, ready for a meal, a solemn meal, i.e., the Last Supper.

During this meal Jesus did something new, something that had never been done before at a solemn meal. He spoke three very important sentences during this meal, sentences that are as important as the words at the time of creation: "Let there be light."

a. He said of the bread in his hands: "This is my body" (T and drawing: bread plate and bread). If the apostles had been able to

see, they would have noticed that the cup began to shine (in the drawing, rays around the cup).

c. What does this mean? The bread has been changed into the body of Jesus. The wine has been changed into his blood. And when the apostles ate the bread, they ate for the first time the "holy bread". This was their first communion.

d. Finally Jesus spoke the third sentence, a command: "Do this in memory of me!" This means that the apostles were to do exactly the same thing he had done.

APPLICATION. The next time we go to Mass, let us look carefully and see whether the same thing happens as happened at the Last Supper. If it does, the church becomes another Last Supper room ("Upper Room"), and the Mass is the same as the Last Supper. And we are allowed to be there just as the apostles were at that time. How do you think they felt? How will you feel the next time you go to Mass?

"DO THIS . . .!"

AIM. To understand the structure of the Mass as a meal, and to see that it is identical with the Last Supper, even though the form has changed.

PREPARATION. Did you pay careful attention at Mass last Sunday, and notice that it is the same as the Last Supper? Today we shall see not only what is the same, but also what is different.

PRESENTATION. Make yourselves comfortable in your chairs and close your eyes. We can still see – those things which we imagine to ourselves. Now imagine our church: the church door – we enter – genuflect – go to our seat – fold our hands – look at the altar. It is like being at a movie. We shall look only at the most

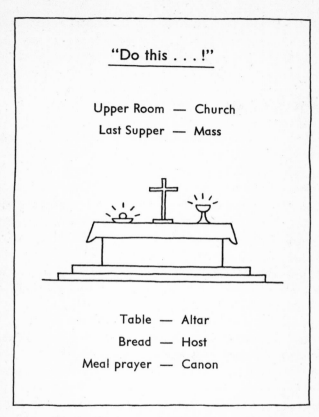

"Do this . . . !"

Upper Room — Church
Last Supper — Mass

Table — Altar
Bread — Host
Meal prayer — Canon

important things: the servers bring the gifts (ciborium[1] with
the bread, and water and wine). The priest takes them, pours wine
and water into the chalice, and now the table is ready with the

---

[1] In some churches the ciborium is replaced by a communion bowl. A cup is
used for drinking, a plate or bowl is used for eating. We should take the
language of things seriously.

gifts: bread and wine. We see the priest praying alone – the meal prayer – suddenly he genuflects and lifts up the host, then the chalice, while all the people look up at it. And now the people leave their seats and go up to the altar, and the priest gives them the holy bread, from the ciborium. Open your eyes!

EXPLANATION. All this is the same as at the Last Supper – but other things are different. We shall write them down and draw them.

a. The Upper Room is our church (T). We do not say "Last Supper", but "the Mass" (T). The table has a different shape, it stands on steps and is called "altar" (T). The bread is white and thin and round and is called "host" (T). There are many hosts in the ciborium (drawing: altar – ciborium with host – chalice).

b. The meal prayer is called "Canon". During it the priest speaks the three important sentences: "This is my body." At the same time he genuflects and lifts up the host, and if we could now see as angels see, we would notice that the bread begins to shine (T: rays around the host). "This is my blood." If we could see as angels see, we would notice that the chalice begins to shine (T: rays around the chalice). "Do this in memory of me." Bread and wine are transformed. Jesus does this from heaven.

c. Now everything in our drawing is as it was at the Last Supper, only the form has changed a little. The cross which stands on the altar is still missing (drawing). We shall talk about it in our next class.

APPLICATION. When we go to Mass we obey the command of Jesus, "Do this" (T). Is this a difficult command, or does it not also sound like an invitation to a feast? That is why, for 2000 years now, Christians everywhere in the world have set up this table, called "altar", and gather around it in obedience and joy – a multitude so great that it cannot be counted. And whenever you go to Mass, you too belong to this multitude.

". . . IN MEMORY OF ME"

AIM. This lesson on the Mass is based on the twofold concept of "form and execution", i.e., he who executes the form of the meal is drawn into the sacrifice. This relationship is made apparent to the children through the correspondence of the three drawings.

PREPARATION. If we are to understand today's lesson well, we must first consider a comparison. I shall draw two picture frames on the board (only the squares are drawn). Now let us imagine that these are two negatives of photographs, which are then both printed together on the third picture (draw the third square). Have you ever seen such a photo? It is called "double exposure". (Most of the children will be familiar with it from photography, or from a magazine.) Now we shall do the same thing with the drawings.

PRESENTATION AND EXPLANATION. a. We know what the first picture represents – "the Last Supper" (T). What have I drawn? (Table made ready, plate with bread and cup, and rays – explain the drawing in these words.)

b. The second picture we shall call "the bloody sacrifice of the cross". (T. Since it too is familiar to the children, the different elements are worked out together with them.)

c. And now let us put both pictures into the third, which is called "the Mass" (T). Look at it carefully, to see if everything is there: the steps (this is the hill) – the altar made ready (table) – the ciborium with hosts – the chalice – the rays.

d. Is the Last Supper contained in the Mass? Yes! (Drawing: arrow.) Who can now tell us what the Mass is? The Mass is the Last Supper, with this difference: not only once and in Jerusalem, but always and everywhere. We say: "The Mass is a meal" (T).

e. What is yet missing from the second picture? The hill (= steps) – body and blood are already here (separated, as on the cross).

The cross is still missing. On every altar there stands a cross. And now the second picture too is contained in the third. Perhaps, then, there is in the Mass not only the Last Supper, but also the sacrifice of the cross? (Drawing: second arrow.) With this difference: not painfully, but without blood. Who can tell us now what the Mass is, in addition to the Last Supper? The Mass is also the sacrifice of the cross. We shall therefore write: "The Mass is a meal and a sacrifice" (complete drawing on board). This sentence is short, you can easily remember it.

APPLICATION. If someone were to ask you: "What is the Mass?", would you be able to answer him? You will tell him of the Last Supper and of the sacrifice of the cross.

One thing is very important for us right now: When we are at Mass, it is as though we were in the Upper Room and on Calvary. During Mass we think of what Jesus did in the Upper Room, and of what he did on Calvary. That is why he said: Do this . . . "in memory of me" (T).

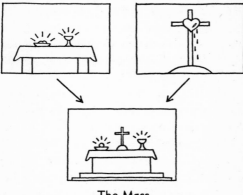

"...in memory of me!"

The Last Supper

The bloody Sacrifice
of the Cross

The Mass

The Mass is a meal and a sacrifice

THE STRUCTURE OF THE MASS

AIM. The structure of the Mass should help the children, like a "program", to find their way through this complicated celebration. (In a slow class this lesson may be omitted. In general, however, it is well worth implanting firmly in the children's minds, already at this stage, the Mass structure – for the sake of their remaining years in school, as well as for later life.)

PREPARATION. If your school has a big celebration, all the guests receive a program. The program tells them the order of events and what they are to do, so that they can participate more fully in the celebration.

If we are invited to come to Mass and to participate in the celebration, we too must know our way around; we need a program, and we call it "the structure of the Mass" (T).

PRESENTATION. A "structure" is made up of different parts. There are, first of all, two main parts of the Mass:

1. The word service. 2. The eucharistic celebration. (T, Practice these words right away.) The eucharistic celebration has three parts (drawing: scheme with the Roman numerals).

EXPLANATION. a. The first main part is the "word service", that is, we serve God with the word, which we speak, pray, read, sing, hear; e.g., when we pray the *Kyrie,* or the great prayer of praise called *Gloria,* or when the Gospel is read to us. The word service is made up of many different parts, you need not yet learn how many. If you are very attentive at Mass over a period of time you will notice how one part follows the other.

b. But you must learn quite thoroughly that the second main part, the eucharistic celebration, is made up of three parts: first the table is prepared (T: preparing the table) – then the meal prayer

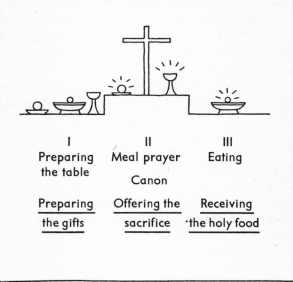

The Structure of the Mass

1. Word Service
2. Eucharistic Celebration

I	II	III
Preparing the table	Meal prayer	Eating
	Canon	
Preparing the gifts	Offering the sacrifice	Receiving the holy food

is spoken (T) – then we eat (T). Now let us find more solemn names for all this!

c. During the preparation of the table we see bread and wine being prepared (drawing: paten and ciborium with hosts and chalice).

That is why we say, more solemnly, "Preparing the gifts" (T).

d. Next we shall take the third part, because it is simple. Instead of "eating", we say: "Receiving the holy food." (T. Drawing: ciborium with hosts.)

e. During the meal prayer the priest gives thanks for the meal, he prays in thanksgiving. The Greek word for this is *eucharist*. While the priest speaks this prayer we notice that something happens suddenly: he genuflects, because the bread has been changed into the body and the wine into the blood of Christ (drawing: host and chalice with rays). The meal prayer (T: Canon) is like a veil beneath which the change takes place. This is called the "consecration".

f. But during the consecration something else happens as well: the body and blood of Christ are now present separately on the altar, just as they were on Calvary, where Jesus offered the sacrifice of the cross. That is why we now say: during the consecration Jesus offers the sacrifice. (Drawing of the cross, and "Offering the sacrifice".)

APPLICATION. If we have learned this structure very well, it is much easier for us really to participate in the Mass. For when we understand what is going on it does not seem so long, and we are glad to have a part in it. That is how I want it to be for you the next time you go to Mass.

PREPARING THE GIFTS

AIM. The next three lessons deal with the three parts of the eucharistic celebration. Starting with the function of each, we ask the question: What should we be doing at this time? It is the meaning of each part, rather than the Mass texts, that will lead us to a generally valid attitude of prayer – an attitude which, while making us independent of a prayer book or missal, will also give us the key for understanding them.

PREPARATION. We shall now learn very carefully what we must do at Mass in order to be able to share in the celebration as we should, and with our whole heart.

PRESENTATION. If you are invited to a feast you prepare yourself: you make sure that your clothes are clean and mended. But these are only external preparations. The Mass is also a feast, but external preparations here are not enough. A clean suit – a neat dress – these are important, but they only remind us that our soul too must be clean. The preparation of the soul, the interior preparation, is what really counts.

EXPLANATION. We must look into our heart and make it ready, both before Mass and during it.

1. Before Mass. I clean my soul – either by going to confession, or by asking God for forgiveness the night before. We shall learn more about this later (T: confession – contrition).

2. Fasting is part of the preparation. The Church prescribes that we must be "empty" when we eat the holy bread, and we call this "fasting". That is why we must stop eating three hours before, and drinking one hour before. Water, however, we may drink up to the moment Mass begins.

3. Next, in church. During the word service we do our best to join in the praying and singing (T).

4. When the priest reads the Gospel and afterwards explains it in the sermon we listen carefully, because it is the Word of God (T).

5. Now comes the first part of the eucharistic celebration: the table is prepared. The gifts of bread and wine are brought to the altar by the servers. The host which you took from the basket (plate) as you entered the church and placed in the ciborium now lies in it, on the altar (drawing).[1]

What does this mean? If your host could talk as it lies on the altar, so close to God, what would it say to him, very softly?

> With all that I do
> I give you my day,
> my talking and thinking,
> my work and my play![2]

And if a part of "you" is in the host, then it would mean "you", it would represent your heart. Now you know, too, what to pray as you place your host in the ciborium. And while the servers carry it to the altar we sit quietly and watch, and each of us prays in his heart: "With all that I do I give you my day . . .". All these

---

[1] We are referring here to the growing practice of having a table at the entrance to the church, with a basket or plate full of unconsecrated hosts, a spoon and the ciborium (or communion bowl), in which there already lies the large host; the cruets for water and wine also stand on the table. All who wish to receive communion place a host from the basket in the ciborium.

[2] Other suggestions: "I give myself to you with my body and soul" – "I want to be yours with all that I have", etc. It is advisable to teach the children a short sentence by heart, since this will help them to be collected. But whatever the words, they should have the right orientation: "Like Jesus, doing the will of the Father", so that little by little the entire life-plan of the children, as well as of the adults, can "flow" into these words.

106

Preparing the Gifts

1. I clean my soul
   (confession — contrition)
2. Fasting
3. Praying and singing
4. We hear the Word of God
5. Preparing the table —
   preparing the heart

With all that I do
I give you my day,
my talking and thinking,
my work and my play!

prayers too are being carried up to the altar. If only we could see it!

Now you understand that your host stands for your heart. It is not only bread and wine which are the gifts on the altar, but also all our hearts. And we remember: preparing the table = preparing our heart (T).

APPLICATION. Let us see whether we can give this day also to God: "With all that I do . . .": Does God like what you have done so far today? If what we did was good, our gift will please him. What else will you be doing today? After school – at home – when you are playing – in the evening . . .?

A suggestion: Let us practice this afternoon "doing all that we do" in such a way that God will be pleased. Before going to sleep tonight let us all pray the prayer of preparing our heart: "With all that I do I give you my day", i.e., we want to give to God the day just *past*. How many will join in this? This is a practice, an exercise. In doing it we are practicing what we shall do in the morning, the next time we go to Mass and receive holy communion – giving to God the day which is *coming*.

OFFERING THE SACRIFICE

AIM. To have the children clearly understand that beneath the veil of the meal prayer Christ offers his sacrifice to the Father, and that we join him in our "prayer at the elevation".

PREPARATION. There is a great deal to see during Mass. If we watch very carefully we shall understand the invisible meaning of everything, e.g.: we see the table being prepared – but the preparing of our heart happens invisibly inside us.

At one moment during the Mass the priest lifts something up to God the Father. What is the invisible meaning of this?

PRESENTATION. We already know that during the meal prayer the consecration takes place. The servers ring the bell and we see

Offering the Sacrifice

Meal prayer → Elevation → Sacrifice

**Accept, heavenly Father, the body
of our Lord Jesus Christ, which
was given for us on the cross**

**Accept, heavenly Father, the blood
of our Lord Jesus Christ, which
was shed for us on the cross**

the priest genuflect and lift the consecrated bread high up – for a few moments. Then he lifts up the chalice too, with the consecrated wine (drawing: the large host and the chalice with rays). This lifting up is called the "elevation".

EXPLANATION. If we understand the invisible meaning of this, we can pray along with the priest.

1. It is good that we can see the holy, consecrated gifts, so that we can look at them reverently – but this is not yet the most important thing.

2. To *whom* does the priest lift the holy bread? It is as though he were handing the holy gifts invisibly to God the Father – giving them to him – as a present – as an offering.

Now we understand: the lifting up means that Christ offers his gifts, his body and blood, to God the Father. He offers the sacrifice (T: "sacrifice" and title).

3. This is a very holy moment, like the sacrifice of the cross on Calvary. The door to heaven is open invisibly, and through it Christ, invisibly, passes his gifts in his surrender. What should we do while this is happening?

4. When *Jesus* does something, *we* should be very still, we should look on with great love and think: now Jesus is offering the sacrifice. For me, for all of us.

5. What Jesus does he does for us. And now, here is something very wonderful: we can join him, his gifts are meant to be our gifts too. We are meant to offer together with him and to ask God the Father to accept these gifts. This means that we do the same as Jesus does. And the lifting up of the host and of the chalice do not only mean that Jesus offers, but that we too should offer, along with him.

APPLICATION. 1. Now we know what to do while the sacrifice is being offered. Before the priest lifts up the host and while he bows down, we pray in our hearts: "Accept, heavenly Father, the body of our Lord Jesus Christ . . ." (T). And then we look with love

110

at the consecrated host as it is being lifted up, and know: now it is happening!

Before the chalice is lifted up we pray in the same way: "Accept, heavenly Father, the blood of our Lord Jesus Christ . . ." (T). Then we look up and know: now it is happening!

2. This happens every day in our church, in all the Catholic churches of our town or city, and all over the world! Do you realize that this is something very wonderful and mysterious?

NOTE. When the lesson is reviewed in the next class the teacher should ask the children what happens to the small hosts in the ciborium during the consecration, since until now we have spoken only of the large host of the priest, which is lifted up at the elevation. All our hosts too are changed, in just the same way, into holy bread, into holy food.

A far-reaching link can here be made between this early teaching on the Mass and later eucharistic instruction. In offering his sacrifice, Christ takes our gift, which we have placed on the altar in the symbol of the host, along with his into the next world. The spiritual movement of preparing our hearts flows into the invisible movement of Christ, as rivulets flow into the river. "Brother, take your brothers along" – these words from one of Hölderlin's poems about the river make vivid the invisible movement that is taking place here.

RECEIVING THE HOLY FOOD

INTRODUCTION. Eating the holy food – which is at the same time encounter with our Lord – requires great refinement of soul. The foundation for it should be laid as early as possible, for experience teaches that it will determine later eucharistic piety. During the actual communion procession the *objective* concept of eating a holy food and of being fed with heavenly bread will predominate, since it corresponds to what happens externally at the meal and will help the children to observe the proper gestures in walking, etc. Once they have returned to their seats, however, the *personal* aspect should determine their attitude in prayer. My soul is like an open cup in which Christ, the light, shines and is effective. (The ancient symbol of the open cup represents the "Orante" posture.)

Nothing should block this divine working in me, not even my own praying, however fervent. To open myself entirely to God's working in me, like a prism which is wholly shot through with light, or like a flower which turns toward the sun – such a passive, meditative attitude toward God is very necessary for us western peoples, who are so active and prone to extroversion. Not to pray – not to say anything – but solely to concentrate on the imperceptible working of God in me = silent adoration. To cultivate and practice this attitude is much more important than all the many communion prayers. For in later years, when we receive communion more frequently, perhaps even daily, this will often be all that we are capable of, in the dullness and weariness of the soul. Only after we have exposed ourselves for some time to the divine efficacy does our personal talking with Jesus begin.

AIM. The children should learn very thoroughly a scheme in five points, thanks to which they will be able to go to communion without the interfering aid of a book.

PREPARATION. We have already seen several times that all that is visible at Mass points to something invisible. So too, eating the holy bread points to an invisible reality.

112

The Holy Food

1. Silent adoration
2. Greeting . . . . . .
3. Thanksgiving . . .
4. Petition . . . .
5. Intention . . . . . .

His face is like the sun
shining in its power

PRESENTATION. A man is walking along the road hungry, tired and discouraged; he can hardly keep on going. At long last someone gives him a piece of bread. There is a power in the bread which spreads through his whole body as he eats

113

The Last Supper

This is my body
This is my blood

Do this
in memory of me

see as angels see, they would have noticed that the bread now began to shine (drawing: golden rays around the bread).

b. Of the wine in the cup he said: "This is my blood" (T and drawing of the cup). If the apostles had been able to see as angels

it. He notices that the bread nourishes him, because he is no longer so tired, he has new courage to keep going, at least a little distance.

EXPLANATION. 1. When we eat the "holy bread" a power enters into us too. If we could see as angels see, we would notice that the holy bread shines. (Drawing: the open cup as symbol of a receptive attitude, and the shining Christ-symbol on the host.) We know that these rays are rays of life and joy. They come from the risen Christ. "His face is like the sun shining in its power" (Apoc. 1:16).

What should we pray while this is happening? Nothing, let us only think: Jesus, shine into my body to my very fingertips, so that it will receive resurrection powers – shine into my soul, into that part of it where my love for you is – where my good qualities are (that they may grow) – where my faults are (that they may become less) – where I am happy and where I am sad – where my dreams and desires are – where I am all alone. Now let us practise this. Close your eyes, put your hands in front of your face. (The catechist repeats what he has just said.) I want you to practise this every evening before you go to sleep. (During the next few classes this practice should be repeated, so that the children begin to feel at home in this way of praying.)

This is the first thing we do when we return to our seats. We call it "silent adoration" (T).

2. Only now do we talk with Jesus. We greet him (T: greeting), e.g.: "O great and holy Lord! – My Saviour! – Light of the world!" Think of such a greeting yourself and write it into your workbook – in a secret code, maybe, because no one but Jesus should know what you tell him! After our silent adoration we pray this greeting quietly in our heart, three times.

114

3. Then we thank him (T: Thanksgiving), e.g.: "Jesus, I thank you for coming to me – for dying on the cross – for having risen from the dead – for working the miracle of the multiplication of the loaves ...". Choose one of these or make up your own, and write it into your workbook (again in a code). This too we shall pray three times.

4. Jesus is now in your heart, he hears all that you say, and you can ask him for something. For what? This we must decide already the day before, otherwise we won't be able to think of it at the time, e.g.: "Jesus, I beg you to make my mother well – please see to it that my father starts going to church again – that I may be faithful to you ..." You can ask for anything that is good. Maybe some.-thing is making you sad – write it down, in a beautiful sentence, in your workbook – again in code. Only Jesus must hear it! Repeat your petition three times.

5. This petition will be different for each of us. But now I want to confide to you one which we all share in common, one which we all have at heart, we call it "intention". E.g.: "Dear Lord, I beg you to bring one of the men in our parish back to the faith." I, your teacher, know this man and need your help in praying for him. Or: "Lord, we beg you that there will be no war." (There is scarcely a more powerful help for prayer than a group of children who bring such intentions to the Mass. The intention is written on the board and into each workbook. The catechist should suggest and confide to the children a different intention every two weeks, until they are able to make general intentions on their own.)

APPLICATION. With the help of a railing we can manage to climb the stairs even with eyes closed. So too, if you learn these five points very well, they will help you like a railing, and you will be able to pray without having to look at a book during communion time.

Homework: Practise these five points every evening.

NOTE. In reviewing this lesson, prayers from the missal can be discussed with the children. If the distribution of holy communion takes some time, so that the children have gone through the five points (they may be repeated three times), they can pray these prayers, alone or together: e.g., the commentator says: "Let us turn to page ... and pray together (he prays the first sentence). ... Now we continue quietly. ..." Such a way of praying is very useful, and is a direct guide to private prayer.

THE POWER OF THE HOLY FOOD

INTRODUCTION. The lessons which follow introduce the children to the role of the eucharist in the Christian life, and open their eyes to a correct evaluation of frequent communion.

AIM. To arrive at motives for frequent communion, by understanding the effect of communion.

PREPARATION. A remedy for sickness is called "medicine"; it has a specific effect. If we take it frequently the effect grows. The "holy bread" is also a medicine, a "heavenly medicine". What effect does it have?

PRESENTATION. (The three drawings: three inter-locking rings, a many-colored bouquet of flowers, and a heart with the Christ-symbol.)

EXPLANATION. 1. Do you remember when we drew the three rings for the first time? When Jesus promised the holy bread. He said: "Whoever eats of *this* bread will live forever" (T). The

The Power of the Holy Food

He who receives the body of the Lord
will live forever,

has the will and power to do good,

and is intimately united with Jesus.

He who eats my flesh abides in me, and I in him!

holy bread is, therefore, the "medicine of immortality". This is a
marvelous effect for the future!

2. What is the meaning of the flowers we have drawn? When the
sun shines on them with its warm rays, the buds break forth in

many-colored blossoms. In our soul, also, our good powers open like buds, and we now have the will and power to do good (T). Do you think that we need this effect of the holy bread?

3. Who can explain the third drawing? The heart represents your heart. The Christ-symbol shows that Christ comes into your heart, that Jesus and you are intimately united, deep down in your heart. He has said: "He who eats my flesh abides in me, and I in him!" (T). Do you like being so close to Jesus? It is not always easy. But the better you come to know him, during the years in school and later as an adult, the more you will long for this effect of the holy bread: union with Jesus.

APPLICATION. This bread is a marvelous medicine. But we must treat such a precious thing with great care. We may eat it frequently only if we appreciate it; otherwise it could happen that we eat this holy bread just like any other bread, without thinking, without noticing the difference. If this happens we should fast for a while, until we appreciate it again. If we have to go without ordinary bread for a long time, we realize all over again how good bread tastes!

THE GREAT SECRET

AIM. To show our union with Christ and with each other, as given in the eucharist, through the parable of the vine and the branches.

PREPARATION. Do you know how strangers become real friends? By sharing an important experience. This gives them something in common, it unites them. Now I am going to tell you a great secret; he who knows it will find anywhere in the world people who have something in common with him, so that he and they belong mysteriously together.

The Great Secret

I am the vine

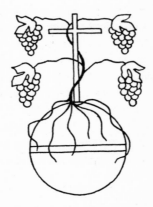

You are the branches

PRESENTATION. (The drawing of the vine. It is the most difficult drawing in the book. Draw first the circle and cross – "the
circle is the world held imprisoned, the cross is salvation and ran-
som." The roots encircle the whole earth, the vine climbs up on the

cross. If the catechist practises this drawing a few times at home on paper, he will be able to execute it quite well on the board. The children like to draw this symbol in many splendid colors.) Also the words of Jesus: I am the vine, you are the branches (T).

EXPLANATION. 1. Roots – vine – branches – grapes – all these belong together. They form one whole, the vine.

2. Although the grapes and the roots are far apart, they have something in common: the same life-sap flows in both.

3. Jesus says that this is a parable, a comparison, which teaches us that all who eat the life-power of Christ in the holy bread belong together, just as everything on the vine belongs together.

4. If we meet a stranger far away from home and realize that he belongs to this vine, he will no longer be a stranger; we shall be united with him as in a pact in which Christ is the Lord. Perhaps you will have to be far away from home some day when you are grown up; then you will realize what a wonderful thing it is to belong to this vine. In all of us there flows the same life-power which is contained in the "holy bread".

5. If someone goes to communion only very rarely, or no longer at all, he will become thin and dry, just like a branch in which there is no longer any life-power. Do you know what Jesus threatened would happen to such a person? He will be cut off like a dead branch and thrown away! To be thrown away by Jesus – can you imagine such a thing?

6. But he who belongs to the vine can bring forth good fruit. The life-power of Christ will be at work in him and will help him to do things in his life which are like precious grapes. And just as grapes give us pleasure, so too such a person gives pleasure to God.

APPLICATION. So you see that what began the day of your first holy communion should continue to grow all your lives – because it unites you with the whole world (look at the drawing!) – because it is important for the whole round earth. The drawing is like a symbol of this secret. Which of you would like to draw it at home in beautiful colors and hang it over your bed for a time?

HOW OFTEN DO I EAT THE HOLY BREAD?

INTRODUCTION. The teaching on the frequency of holy communion is set between two poles. The first is the desire of the Church to see her children as often as possible at the table of the Lord. The principles for this are put on the board to serve as a constant invitation, while leaving room for a free decision. They are the necessary consequence of the realization that the Mass is meal *and* sacrifice, and that participation in the meal is an integral part of the Mass. This should be firmly impressed on the children – notwithstanding the practice to the contrary which still prevails here and there. On the other hand, we should use some restraint in guiding the children to receive communion frequently: because they so quickly "become used to it" – because they do not yet have the necessary capacity to participate in the Mass personally, unless it is a special children's Mass – because experience teaches that zeal grows cold after some years, when the adolescents no longer take seriously their "pious childhood" – because in so many homes there is no longer that Christian atmosphere which the young person would need as protection to his growth.

The teacher will fluctuate between the two poles. He should direct the class as a whole toward the customary monthly or bi-monthly communion; but at the same time, he should constantly strive to direct the children individually to more frequent communion. The diagram can then be completed with: "4. My resolution: . . . ."

AIM. Simple rules for the frequent reception of holy communion.

PREPARATION. Different people receive holy communion more or less often. What differences have you noticed? All of you should know the rules for receiving communion, so that you will be able to decide for yourselves how often you should go.

PRESENTATION. You hear the church bells ringing every Sunday (drawing). If we listen to them very carefully we shall understand their call: Come – come! This is not an order, but an invitation. We either do not listen to it, or we follow it. The invitation does not force us, but it calls us every Sunday.

EXPLANATION. 1. Jesus too invites us – just like the bells – not only to go to Mass, but also to receive communion during Mass. It is not an obligation, but an invitation. Since the time of Pope St. Pius X more and more people are following this invitation.

2. This pope laid down certain rules, so that we would know exactly when and how often we may go to communion: 1. Must. . . . 2. Should. . . . 3. May. . . . (T).

3. Must we go to confession every time before going to communion, if we go more often than once a year? No. We learned during our lessons on confession how often we should go to confession. The conditions for communion are different:

a. I must have the grace-life in me (T). Anyone who loses it – through a very big and terrible sin – must go to confession before receiving communion.

b. I must have the right intention (T). It is possible to have a wrong intention, e.g., in order to please the teacher, so that I will be first in my class. To go to communion frequently for such a

How Often Do I Eat the Holy Bread?

1. Must: once a year — at Easter time — commandment of the Church

2. Should: each Sunday and holy day

3. May: every day

Conditions:

a) I must have the grace-life
b) I must have the right intention

reason is wrong. The *right* intention would be, for instance: in order that I may have eternal life – will and power to do good – that I may be united with Jesus. You remember our lesson – the power of the holy food?

APPLICATION. And now, at the end of class, let us draw an old-fashioned oil lamp. What can happen to such a lamp? It can run out of oil. Therefore, we must remember to fill it in good time. What do you think people resolved to do in those days? To fill their lamps too soon, rather than too late.

Is this principle valid for us too, so that the light in our soul will not go out? The holy bread nourishes the light of grace in us. Now make up your mind how soon you will again go to communion. This coming Sunday? Have you fulfilled the conditions? I should like you to check yourselves on this each Saturday night before you go to sleep.

THE MOST HOLY SACRAMENT OF THE ALTAR

INTRODUCTION. This last lesson is intended to teach the children the veneration of the blessed sacrament. The catechist should realize that children have the capacity to grasp what is great, and that, in explaining great things to them, we need not make them small and pretty. The mistakes that have been made in this respect, and are still being made, in our prayer books and holy cards (the "little Jesus", "the lonely little hermit in the tabernacle", etc.) are obstacles to becoming spiritually mature.

AIM. Factual knowledge about the reservation of the blessed sacrament for the sick, and stimulating the children to venerate it.

PREPARATION. If you enter a strange church, how can you tell whether or not it is Catholic? The red light, the sanctuary lamp. What does it tell us?

PRESENTATION. You are all alone in church. Suddenly the priest comes in, dressed not in the Mass vestments, but in a black suit.

He goes up to the tabernacle (T), unlocks the door, takes out the ciborium (T, word and drawing; also the ciborium veil and the cover). The priest takes out a host and places it in a small locket which he hangs around his neck inside a case (the catechist can

draw a pyx burse). Then he locks the tabernacle again and leaves the church. He goes to someone who is sick and brings him the "holy bread".

EXPLANATION. 1. There are some hosts left over at Mass. These are kept in the ciborium, for the sick who cannot come to church. We call this "holy communion for the sick" (T). If we know of someone who is sick, seriously or for a long time, we should tell the priest about him, so that he can visit the sick person and tell him about this.

2. We have a great treasure in our church. It is called "the most holy sacrament of the altar" (T). The sanctuary lamp tells us: Be silent, you are not alone in church, the body of Jesus, Jesus himself is here. As we pass the tabernacle we genuflect, as a sign of adoration. It is better still to kneel down in front of the tabernacle and to talk with Jesus. We call this "making a visit" (T).

3. At Benediction (T) on Sunday, or sometimes on week days in the evening, people come together to adore this "most holy sacrament of the altar". The priest takes the ciborium from the tabernacle, puts a host inside the "monstrance", and places the monstrance on the altar so that everyone can see it. And now the people pray and sing, as though they were kneeling before the throne of the glorified Lord: "Therefore let us, humbly bending, this great sacrament adore" (Tantum ergo – T).

APPLICATION. There are two things I should like you to do:

1. I want each of you to "make a visit", all alone. How will you do it? (Discussion).

2. I want you all to come to Benediction on one of the coming Sundays. (And now we shall look up in the parish hymn book the hymns which are sung during Benediction.)

Confirmation

The lessons on confirmation which follow are intended as imme-
diate preparation for receiving this sacrament. Of the five instruc-
tions which serve as introduction into the mystery of confirmation,
special attention should be given to the third lesson, which trans-
mits what is most essential in the teaching on confirmation.

Once again our starting point is the external form, which enables
us to grasp the essence of the sacrament and to deduce in broad lines
the interior happenings.

CONFIRMATION MEANS STRENGTHENING

AIM. The right ordering of what the children already know about
confirmation, and focusing it on the essentials; at the same time
the administration of the sacrament is explained.

PREPARATION. Today we begin our lessons on confirmation;
but I wonder whether all of you will really want to keep on
with them to the end? For we cannot receive this sacrament in
the same way in which we received baptism, as a little child or
baby, but should receive it only if we are willing to take on a
certain task. Confirmation gives us strength – "confirms" us – for
this task. Confirmation means strengthening (T). We shall see
whether all of you really want to take on this task.

PRESENTATION. What do you know about confirmation – not
about the day of confirmation, but about the sacrament itself?
Let us think about the most important thing: the bishop comes –
how do we recognize him? (Draw and explain mitre and staff.)
What does the bishop do? (The catechist should slowly "perform"

127

the act of confirmation on a child, with the help of an older child as sponsor – without, of course, the oil and anointing.)

EXPLANATION. Three things belong together in confirmation. Two of them we can see, the third we can hear.

1. "The bishop lays his hand on the candidate" (T) – the bishop touches you.

2. "He anoints his forehead with chrism" (T) – you are anointed with holy oil. (Diagram: plate with vessel of oil. Explain the word "chrism" = anointing with oil, its components = olive oil and balsam, its consecration on Holy Thursday.)

3. While he does this he pronounces the words: "N. N., I sign you . . ." (T).

APPLICATION. This is the most important thing that happens on the day of your confirmation. Everything else is only the setting, which should "fit" the sacrament just as a frame "fits" the picture. (Discuss their confirmation day with the children – how it should be, and how it should not be – and explain the task of the sponsor. Mention the different ways in which the day can be celebrated and urge the children to tell their sponsor already now how they would like to spend the day. In this way abuses can be avoided, and the wishes of the children can be given direction.)

Confirmation Means Strengthening

The bishop lays his hand on the candidate and anoints his forehead with chrism.

This is accompanied by the words:
"John, I sign you with the sign of the cross, and I confirm you with the chrism of salvation, in the name of the Father, and of the Son, and of the Holy Spirit."

THE BISHOP

AIM. To experience the handing on of the full power of consecration across the centuries back to Christ, through the meeting with the bishop (ordinarily the only direct meeting in one's life), especially through the laying on of hands.

PREPARATION. To meet an important and powerful person (e.g., the president, king, or pope) is always a great event in one's life. People talk about it for a long time afterwards. Your meeting with the bishop in confirmation has a very great and special meaning. In each of you something *happens* during this meeting.

PRESENTATION. Let us imagine that Christ were to stretch out his hand from heaven and touch us. This would be a miracle, we would be afraid, we would not know what the consequences will be. But one thing at any rate is certain: we would never be able to forget it, we would be joined with him all our life long. We know that Christ does not do this, but something like this happens in confirmation.

EXPLANATION. Christ breathed on the apostles and gave them the Holy Spirit, on the evening of the day of his resurrection (John 20:22. Diagram: Christ-symbol – key = apostle).

This happened nearly 2000 years ago. In those days the apostles laid their hands on devout and holy men and passed on to them the gift of the Holy Spirit which they had received from Christ. These men were called "bishops" (diagram: bishop's staff).

These bishops in turn passed on their gift and consecrated other men as bishops by laying their hands on them; and this happened again and again, down to our own bishop who comes to us for confirmation. When he touches you it is almost *as if* an apostle were touching you, since he is a successor of the apostles (T).

The Bishop

The bishop is the successor of the apostles and the bearer of the Holy Spirit

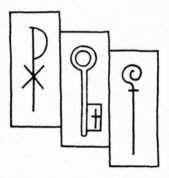

Through the hand of the bishop the power of the Holy Spirit streams down upon me

It is almost "as if" – but one thing is not only "as if", but real and certain: our bishop has the same gift of the Holy Spirit which the apostles received from Christ. "He is the bearer of the Holy Spirit" (T). When he touches you, the power of the Holy Spirit streams down upon you through his hand (T)!

APPLICATION. That is why the meeting with the bishop in confirmation is so important, even exciting. Look at him carefully when your turn comes to be confirmed – there is something in him of the time of Christ, nearly 2000 years ago. All your life you will remember your confirmation day.

BEING STRENGTHENED WITH THE HOLY SPIRIT

AIM. The mystery of confirmation is explained through the events that took place at the "Baptism of Jesus" in the Jordan (Mark 1:9–11).

PREPARATION. There are certain days in one's life which are a turning point. Things were different before, then comes a special day, and now a new life begins. In the life of Jesus too there was such a turning point – it will help us to understand the meaning of confirmation.

PRESENTATION. 1. For 30 years Jesus led a hidden life. From the time he was 12 years old, in the temple, the gospels tell us nothing more about him. This was the "hidden" period of his life (T). We can say that he was preparing himself for his task.

2. Then came the turning point. He went to the Jordan, where John the Baptist was calling people to penance. They must change their lives, and as a sign that they would abandon their sinful ways he baptized them. He told them to bathe in the waters of the Jordan, *as if* they could wash away their sins as one washes away dirt. This baptism was not a sacrament, it was a sign that expressed something without words – their desire: we would like to wash away our sins like dirt. And the water of the Jordan became, as it were, "dirty" with all their sins.

132

hidden life ⟶ Jordan ⟶ public life

↓

taking on the task:

Redemption of the world

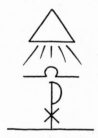

time of preparation ⟶ confirmation ⟶ task in the world

3. And now Jesus came and wanted to be baptized too. At first John did not want to do it. How can Jesus wash away his sins, since he is already clean? But Jesus wanted it this way. His baptism was meant to be a sign, through it he wanted to say something to

God the Father, without words. If someone who is clean washes in dirty water, he becomes dirty himself. And so, when the Sinless One went down into the water of the Jordan, he drew to himself all the dirt of our sins!

When he came up from the water he stood before his Father in heaven laden with the sins of the world. God the Father saw that his Son was saying without words: Now I am ready to begin my task for the world, to take on myself the sins of the world, to begin my office as Messias and Redeemer. The baptism showed that Jesus was willing to begin his task.

4. How does God the Father reply? In two ways. A voice came from heaven: "This is my beloved Son in whom I am well pleased." The Father said that he beholds with joy his Son who is willing to undertake his task.

"The Holy Spirit descended on him in the form of a dove." God the Father sent the Holy Spirit to strengthen Jesus for his difficult task. (The diagram shows what happened: the Son of God on earth = Christ-symbol; God the Father in heaven = the triangle; the Holy Spirit sent by the Father. The symbol of the Holy Spirit can be explained as follows: draw a dove with open wings, then erase the tail and lower part of the wings; this is the ancient Christian symbol of the Holy Spirit.)

5. This was the turning point on the banks of the Jordan – and now a new period began in the life of Jesus. He no longer led a hidden life, he did everything publicly from now on, everyone could see and hear him. That is why we call this new period his "public life" (T).

6. The same thing is repeated in confirmation. The day of confirmation is your turning point. Your "hidden life" is now past – we call it "time of preparation" (T). In "confirmation" (T), the

bishop asks you whether you are ready to take on a task as Christian in the world. This is the promise of confirmation. We shall say more about it at another time. You are confirmed, strengthened for this task with the Holy Spirit, through the laying on of hands and the anointing.

7. The drawing we have made applies also to confirmation. The bishop "plays" the role of God the Father; his vestments shine with a reflection of the glory of God the Father. In the place of Christ (point to the drawing) there stands a Christian boy or girl, ready to take on their task in the world. The Holy Spirit does not appear as dove, however, his power is in the holy oil. After he has anointed you the bishop gently touches your cheek, as if to say: "Now you are my beloved son, my beloved daughter."

So you see that in confirmation something "similar" happens to us as happened to Jesus, we become "like Christ".

APPLICATION. The day of confirmation is a turning point. Now begins your "public life". We call it "task in the world" (T). Should this be a joyful or a serious day? It is in the first place a solemn day, but it is filled with both joy and seriousness too. And this is how your sponsor should celebrate it with you.

MY MISSION

AIM. The task given in confirmation is shown to be great, and at the same time within reach of the children.

PREPARATION. Did you ever have the experience of wanting something very badly – and no chance of getting it? A great goal – and so far away! When this happens our hearts become discouraged. Only one thing can help in such a situation: he who

135

wants to climb a high mountain must start at the bottom and take one step at a time, small steps – but persistent ones; and so he will reach his goal in the end.

It is the same with the task given in confirmation, a task which points in the same direction as the task of Jesus.

PRESENTATION. Do you remember the door of paradise? Men stood outside – the door was closed – no one could enter the place where God was – until the Saviour, Jesus, came and opened the door – and now the separation is no longer there, we can enter. This is a comparison for the task, for the commission, for the mission of Jesus in the world.

EXPLANATION. 1. The door is the door of heaven. It stands between the world and God and separates them from each other. No one can come to God, something is in the way. You know this from our earlier classes: it is the result of the terrible thing that happened in paradise. The closed door of paradise means that there is no passage from God to men.

2. But God the Father sent the Saviour with the task to open the door. This he did on the cross. Since that time the door is open. But he did more still. He showed men also the way to the door – he helped them to find it. If we add all this up and put it together we could say it like this: Jesus had the task to unite men once again with God.

3. This task is not yet ended. Christ went back to heaven, and others had to carry on this task: his Christians. In confirmation the Christian receives the task – to unite men with God. To put it more simply, we say: "to have an effect in the world as Christian" (T).

4. We stand before this task as before a high mountain! We can go about it in the wrong way and in the right way. A great goal and a

My Mission

When I am confirmed I receive the task
to have an effect in the world as Christian.

My sword is the faith,
My shield is fidelity,
My standard is the cross.

small heart! There is nothing for us to do than to set out one step
a time, a small step but the right one.

5. a. The parents of one of your friends don't wake him Sunday
morning in time for church. The two of you agree on a signal, and

you come to get him. This means that you have to get up fifteen minutes early. But you are uniting him with God. A small step – but the right one. (This is concern for others.) To keep it up, won't you need strength through confirmation?

b. A new boy in school seems interested in your religion. You show him your books and notebook, answer his questions, and bring him to church. We call this: showing the way to God with words.

c. In Mary's family there is much speaking against the Church. She can't say anything, for that would only make matters worse. So she makes a visit to church every week and asks Jesus to forgive them. She prays for others – as Jesus did.

d. In the factory where Dick works they use very bad language. Dick tells the man next to him to be quiet. Thereupon some men beat him up. He defends himself, but there are three of them. He bears the pain for the sake of the others! (Reparation)

6. The task of confirmation is often like a battle. For this we need weapons and an armour, like a knight: sword and shield and standard. "My sword is the faith . . .", etc. (T).

7. The older a Christian becomes, the more he can do for his task: pupil – teacher – doctor – statesman – priest – bishop.

APPLICATION. Now you know what is the task which you take on in the promise of confirmation. Will all of you come to be confirmed? Are *you* willing to make the promise? – Every Sunday you are reminded of this by special words – at the end of Mass: Ite – missa est! Go, you are sent! You are sent out into the coming week, there to fulfill your task. This is my mission!

THE GRACE OF CONFIRMATION

AIM. The effect of the grace of confirmation is shown through what happened to St. Peter on the first Pentecost.

PREPARATION. We have resolved to look carefully at the bishop, before our turn comes to be confirmed. But what should you do at the moment when you stand before him and he confirms you? There is a prayer for this!

PRESENTATION. Let us look at St. Peter at Pentecost. We notice that he has become different. Before, he had the doors locked from fear of the Jews. Afterwards, he was no longer afraid, he came out and spoke to the many people who had come together. What caused this change?

"Suddenly there came a sound from heaven, as of a mighty wind coming, and it filled the whole house where they were sitting. And there appeared to them parted tongues of fire, which settled upon each of them. And they were all filled with the Holy Spirit" (Acts 2:3-4). What has happened?

EXPLANATION. 1. Peter and the others are gathered together in the Upper Room. They are supposed to bring the message of Jesus to the ends of the earth – but they do not have the strength for this!

2. Two signs: The Holy Spirit came from heaven through the air, invisibly and with a mighty sound. Inside the room he became visible – this time not as a dove, but as flames of fire which looked like tongues. They spread around the room and alighted on each of the apostles, and the fire entered their hearts: enlightening and burning, like a fierce enthusiasm, so that they can no longer be silent but must speak and act.

3. Where before there was fear, now there is courage. Peter felt

the strength in himself to carry on the task of Christ: to unite the world with God, to have an effect in the world as Christian. He has been strengthened, "confirmed".

4. The same strength is given to us in confirmation, even if we do not feel it the way Peter did on the first Pentecost. This gift we call a grace, the "grace of confirmation" (T). It strengthens us for our task just as it strengthened Peter.

5. This strengthening comes from the Holy Spirit. We know that he is the third divine Person. In the Creed of the Mass he has the title, "Giver of life". He gives life (Genesis: the Spirit of God hovering over the abyss. Annunciation: the Holy Spirit shall come upon you and you shall bear a son). In the hymn *Veni Creator Spiritus* we call on him to "confirm our weak bodies" (T: "Giver of strength").

APPLICATION. 1. What, then, shall we do at the moment when we stand before the bishop and know: now the same thing will happen to me as happened to Peter? We feel the bishop's hand placed on our head, he is anointing us, and we pray in our heart: "Come, Holy Spirit, strengthen me!" (T) We pray this sentence again and again. And in this way we are aware of what is happening, we are paying attention, fervently and intelligently.

2. I want you to pray this confirmation-prayer three times every evening before you go to sleep. That will be like saying: "Come, Holy Spirit, and make me strong on the day of my confirmation!"

The Grace of Confirmation

The Holy Spirit is the third divine Person.

Giver of life — Giver of strength

Come, Holy Spirit, and strengthen me!